' IN AFFECTIONATE REMEM

The Wood Pit Explosion,

Haydock.

7th. June, 1878.

Geoff Simm.

Ian Winstanley.

Published by;-
Picks Publishing, 1992.
83, Greenfields Crescent,
Ashton-in-Makerfield,
Wigan, WN4 8QY.
Lancashire,
Tel. (0942) 723675.

I.S.B.N. 0 9516843 5 3.

Printed by:-

Willow Printing 75/79 Back Cross Lane, Newton-le-Willows, Merseyside WA12 9YE
Telephone: (0925) 222449 or 228524

From a rubbing of a gravestone in St.Thomas' Churchyard, Ashton-in-Makerfield.

IN AFFECTIONATE REMEMBRANCE

OF

Thomas Wood
who was killed in
the Wood Pit Explosion, Haydock.
June 7th. 1878.
Aged 25 Years.

That morning so early when leaving thy home,
We little expected you would not return.
For down that deep coal pit we could not get near,
To sooth the one moment though loved thee so dear.

ACKNOWLEDGMENTS.

The authors wish to express their grateful thanks to;-
St. Helens Local History Library and Archive.
Lancashire National Union of Mineworkers.
Salford Mining Museum.
Norman Boon.
Alan Davies.
Fran Davies.
Tim Griffiths.
Vivien Hainsworth.
Peter Hughes.
Roy Jackson.
Colleen P. Main.

' IN AFFECTIONATE REMEMBRANCE.'

The Wood Pit Explosion,

Haydock.

7th. June, 1878.

' IN AFFECTIONATE REMEMBRANCE.'

The Wood Pit Explosion,

Haydock.

7th. June, 1878.

Authors' Note.

It is about four years since Ian and Geoff first published books on local history, they could not have guessed how much interest they were to arouse in the area and further afield. Copies of '*Weep Mothers Weep*' and '*Richard Evans of Haydock*' have found their way to Canada, Australia, New Zealand and the U.S.A. as well as all over the British Isles. When they wrote '*Mining Memories*' for the St.Helens Mining 1990 Festival, little did they think that the end of deep mining in Lancashire was so close and the title of the book so poignant. With the threatened closure of Parkside, that will be the end of the once great Lancashire coalfield and all that will be left will be memories.

'*Weep Mothers Weep*', which is an account of the Wood Pit Explosion which occurred in Haydock in 1878, was the product of about four years research and caused a great deal of interest. The book contains many details of the victims and had found its way into some unusual places. There is a copy in the State Library, Boston Massatuchets and it has been included in the Mormon Index. Since the publication of the book much new material and information about the disaster has come to light which is so interesting, unique and of such excellent quality, that it warranted another publication which is the subject of this book.

There are surviving relatives of the Boon family who lost seven male members, in the disaster, a complete Subscription List for the Explosion Relief Fund has come to light at the St. Helens Local History Library and Archive, rubbings of gravestones of the victims and best of all, a contemporary photographic record of the disaster taken by one of the Evans family, the owners of the colliery.

These photographs form a very important part of the history of mining, not only in Lancashire, but in the country. In 1878 photography was in its infancy and for the pictures to have survived, to be in such a splendid condition, and to come into the hands of two people that are so interested in the subject, is a very fortunate quirk of fate.

The story of the disaster was alive in the village. Many facts about it had passed into folklore but what had not faded was the memory of the day in June, 1878. At talks that were given on the subject, people would approach us and tell us with a burning pride, tinged with deep sadness, that their grandfather, or one of their relatives had lost their lives in the pit.

The victims of the explosion and their relatives share a sombre part of the history of coal mining in Lancashire and stand as a testament to the true price of coal. It is to their memory that we dedicate this book '*In Affectionate Remembrance*.'

I.G.W., G.S. February, 1993.

John Squires.

JOHN SQUIRES' DIARY.

John Squires was born on the 22nd. August, 1835 in Walton, Liverpool, the son of Richard and Mary Squires. Mary was the daughter of Richard Evans, coal proprietor of Haydock. His father was the owner and master of a private lunatic asylum in Walton and was a respected supporter of the church and community.

John Squires emigrated to New Zealand in 1858 and three years after married Catherine Dewe in Milton, New Zealand. He had previously been to Australia in 1854, working as a stockmen on a cattle ranch. Two of his brothers, Richard Westbrooke and Horace Lyne, followed him to New Zealand but Horace later returned to work in the Haydock Collieries.

At the time of the Wood Pit Disaster, John Squires was 43 years of age. He had returned from New Zealand in 1875 on the invitation of his Uncle Joseph, to assist in the running of the agricultiral interests of Richard Evans and Company. John must have had a keen mind as his Uncle also used him to assist in tracing the family's pedigree. After the death of Uncle Joseph, he became one of the Directors of Richard Evans & Co. Ltd., eventually returning to New Zealand, where he died in 1901.

A large number of his diaries have survived and are in the possession of his descendants in New Zealand. Sections of his diary for 1878, both before and after the Wood Pit Disaster are included here. The entries gives a clear indication of the size and complexity of the family firm, with John travelling all over South Lancashire and North Wales to various meetings. The diary also shows what a close family the Evans' were with visits to and from Aunts, Uncles, Cousins and Brothers. John Squires was a tough, hard working and religious individual, with few feelings about the number of the dead, yet still prepared to canvass for the Weselyans in his spare evenings.

John was involved with the managing of farm estates and had little to do with the Company's mines. The extracts from the diary start the week before the disaster. No one in the village or The Richard Evans Company had any idea of what was in store for the village in the form of the terrible disaster that was to come. Day to day life was going on as normal for John Squires as it was for the men who worked at Wood Pit and their families.

June 2nd. Sunday.   Fine
I drove Aunt Wetherall to Walton Church, and after service we visited all the graves, and then drove to Aunt Norris where we dined and tead and then returned to Haydock.

Aunt Wetherall and Aunt Norris were his father's sisters and Walton, Liverpool, was the family church.

June 3rd. Monday.   Fine.
At office morning and afternoon U.J. there sending off traces to the Land Securities Co.

'Uncle Joseph' was Joseph Evans who was at that time, the sole owner of Richard Evans & Co.

June 4th. Tuesday.   Wet.
At the office. Went to Grange - found Wm. Mee there talking over 'pedigree' with uncle Joseph. Wet afternoon. At home writing 'Evans'. Horaces friend from Blue Spur called. Seymours leg bad.

'Horace' was Horace Lyne Squires, brother to John.

June 6th. Thursday   Fine.
At office. Grange to dinner. Tea at Heyes. Playing bowls and cricket in evening.

'*The Grange*' was the Evans' family home in Haydock and '*The Heyes*' was the home of Lydia Evans, the widow of Josiah.

Friday 7th. June, 1878.   *Fine.*
Dined at Arthur Evans then met Harvie at railway who told us a terrible explosion at Wood pit had occurred. Returned to Haydock, staying at Wood Pit till 10.30 p.m. Supposed that over 200 were dead.

Arthur Evans was Arthur Henry Lyne Evans, the eldest son of Josiah Evans. He took no active part in the running of the Company and was a keen photographer. It was he who took the photographs and compiled the album on the disaster.

'*Harvie*' was Mr. Harvey, the Secretary to Richard Evans & Co. and is referred to on several occasions in the diary. He was no stranger to mining disasters. Major tragedy had last visited the Haydock Collieries on the 21st. July, 1869 when fifty nine men and boys lost their lives in an explosion of firedamp at Queen Pit.

At the time, Mr. Harvey was at work in the Company Offices and was very quickly at the pit head on hearing the news. The pit was just across the road and he organised the first rescue parties to go down the mine.

As the survivors were brought to the surface, many of them suffering from the effects of afterdamp, burnt, or both, he organised twenty three hand carts in which they could be taken to their homes where they were tended by two local doctors, Drs. Jameson and Twyford.

June 8th. Saturday. *Showery.*
At office all day. 21 bodies were recovered and laid out in the cart shed. Busy instituting relief committee &c.,

The official records of the day tell us that as the victims were found, they were numbered and their position marked on a plan. Assuming that the victims mentioned here were the first twenty one on the official list;-

John Molyneaux, 20, dataller.	Joseph Hindley, 13, drawer.
James Higson, 19, wagoner.	Henry Waterworth, 23, dataller.
William Jameson, 15, pony driver.	Thomas Dixon, 48, jigger.
	William Smth, 33, dataller.
Edward Sutton, 15, dataller.	William Smith, 19, dataller.
William Winstanley, 12, coupler.	John Evans, 23, collier.
William Wilcock, 61, dataller.	William Hindley, 12, pony driver.
Thomas Winstanley, 13, pony driver.	Joseph Griffiths, 14, wagoner.
	James Barnes, 30, dataller.
Thomas Shaw, 22, dataller.	John Evans, 14, hooker-on.
James Leyland, 40, collier.	Henry Waterworth, 23, dataller.

June 9th. Sunday
Meeting in morning. At Wesleyian evening.

June 10th. Monday
About the colliery. 40 bodies recovered to this time. Had tea at Grange.
The victims recovered on Saturday and Sunday following the disaster were;-

Edward Waterworth, 23, dataller.	Johnathan Rowley, 35, collier.
Robert Rowland, 20, drawer.	Enoch Booth, 25, collier.
Evan Meredith, 36, collier.	Thomas Pilkington, 26, collier.
John Hindley, 12, jigger.	Daniel Wilson, 19, drawer.

James Whittle, 62, dataller.
Richard Evans, 20, collier.
Thomas Clare, 37, collier.
John Blinstone, 20, drawer.
John Knowles, 23, collier.

James Pierpoint, 17, drawer.
William Turncock, 28, collier.
Thomas Skidmore, 24, drawer.
John Pilling, 24, collier.

June 11th. Tuesday.   *Showery. Thundery.*
About the colliery. very little done at Wood Pit owing to quantity of gas. Towards evening more progress was made and 4 bodies recovered.

The victims recovered were;-
Edward Evans, 40, collier.
Thomas Reed, 36, dataller.

James Fairhurst, 41, collier.
William Fairhurst, 27, dataller.

June 12th. *Wednesday.   Showery.*
At office. At meeting in aid of widows and orphans at Liverpool, Earl of Derby presiding 12 bodies recovered today. Work stopped at 6 p.m. owing to men being tired out.

These would be;-
Thomas Whittle, 20, collier.
James Norbury, 44, collier.
Thomas Waterworth, 22, balancer.
Martin Roach, 22, dataller.
John Mruphy, 17, drawer.

Thomas Arnold, 25, drawer.
Peter Millington, 32, collier.
William Cunnah, 40, collier.
Peter Nolan, 19, drawer.
George Hales, 32, dataller.
James Clifford, 21, dataller.

June 13th. Tuesday.   *Fine.*
At office and Grange. Slow progress made at Wood Pit. Up to this afternoon 80 bodies recovered altogether.

Victims 57 to 80;-
William Dearden, 32, dataller.
James Dearden, 28, jigger.
William McGlynn,16, drawer.
Peter Roach, 22, dataller.
Thomas Wood, 25, bricksetter.
Thomas McCarty, 20, collier.
John Welding, 15, pony driver.
Robert Hughes, 26, drawer.
John Jones, 19, drawer.
Llewellyn Lloyd, 29, collier.
James Thomas, 32, collier.
Daniel Gittens, 35, collier.

Michael Roach, 25, dataller.
Isaac Lloyd, 27, collier.
James Roberts, 15, pony tenter.
John Evans, 14, hooker-on.
Henry Rowley, 13, jigger.
John Jones, 28, collier.
John Edwards, 49, collier.
George Cunliffe, 24, drawer.
William Roberts, 35, collier.
William Boon, 15, drawer.
Isaac Boon, 21, collier.
Thomas Boon, 18, drawer.

June 14th. Friday.   Fine.
At office. Went with Aunty Ruth To Rhyl.
June15th. Saturday.
Returned to Haydock with Aunty Ruth. Found 52 bodies were recovered.

Victims 81 to 133;-

Charles Redman, 26, dataller.
John Jones, 22, dataller.
James Peake, 14, pony driver.
Job Swain, 18, jiggerman.
John Boon, 42, collier.
Edward Richardson, 39, collier.
Thomas Thompson, 28, collier.
Hugh Wade, 21, drawer.
John Cusic, 18, drawer.
James Fox, 27, drawer.
John King, 31, collier.
Thomas Melling, 22, dataller.
George Green, 15, pony driver.
Peter Tyrer, 51, dataller.
James Twiss, 27, collier.
Woodwin Jones, 21, drawer.
Peter Hughes, 37, collier.
John Pimblett, 21, drawer.
Peter Sharples, 35, collier.
Bernard Nolan, 27, collier.
William Leyland, 46, collier.
Joseph Twiss, 22, collier.
James Owen, 14, drawer.
George Danks, 24, dataller.
Matthew Fairhurst, 24, drawer,
Samuel Winstanley, 51, collier.
Joseph Cotterall, 27, dataller.

Robert Ellis, 33, dataller.
Willliam Owen, 12, drawer.
Edward Byron, 16, drawer.
James Bibby, 56, dataller.
James Winstanley, 18, drawer.
John Green, 21, drawer.
Thomas Pimblett, 36, collier.
Thomas Sharples, 41, collier.
Ralph Ashcroft, 21, drawer.
George Morton, 58, dataller.
James Ashcroft, 53, collier.
James Ashcroft, 16, drawer.
James Whittle, 62, dataller.
William Carey, 16, drawer.
Joseph Green, 23, drawer.
John Pimblett, 13, drawer.
William Welding, 21, dataller.
John Redford, 15, pony driver.
James Greenall, 34, collier.
James Dillon, 16, drawer.
John Welding, 36, collier.
John Conway, 20, dataller.
George Powell, 35, dataller.
Edward Pimblett, 43, collier.
James Lyon, 44, dataller.
Edward Rodgers, 37, dataller.

June 16th. Sunday.
Meeting in morning. Dined with Hadfield. Outdoor meeting in afternoon at Lyme Street.

The next entries in the diary were business appointments that had nothing to do with the explosion. The next relevant entry was;-

July 4th. Thursday.   *Thundery.*
The inquest on the bodies began at the Ram's Head. I was there.

July 5th. Friday   *Fine.*
At works and inquest. At office in afternoon with U.J. and Harvie (Harvey). Annie and Bill Evans discussing the salt business Aunt Ruth gave the widows tea at the Grange.

Aunt Ruth was Ruth Evans, daughter of Richard Evans, the colliery proprietor. She was a Victorian lady who was interested in education and held classes for Haydock children. Later she endowed British Schools in Ashton-in-Makerfield and Rhyll and Congregational Churches in Haydock, Ashton and Rainhill. She remained unmarried and was the life-long companion and housekeeper of her brother, Joseph. She died, aged 77 years, in North Wales but was buried at the Congregational Church, Newton-le-Willows.

July 19th. Friday.   *Fine.*
At office. At explosion inquest all day. Went to Grange to tell UJ about the verdict.

July 21st. Thursday.   *Fine.*
Meeting in morning. Dined at Heyes. Wesleyans evening Mr. Kendrew preached on behalf of widows and orphans fund.

The formal verdict read;-
"We believe that there had been a fouling of the air connected with a sudden outburst of gas or a fall of roof, but by whom the gas was ignited there is no evidence to show. The explosion was caused by faulty ventilation and by an accumulation of gas near Evans' place, which had been expelled from thence by a fall of roof, assisted by fouling, which was known to exist previous to the explosion by the fireman and others."

In the light of later knowledge what probably happened was that Evans or Clare holed into a large reservoir of gas in the coal which escaped under such pressure that it probably screamed out. The men, taking fright would naturally have run for their lives against the current of ventilating air. Their badly burnt bodies were found away from their working places and facing the pit bottom. They were the only men that were out of their places. The lamps that they were using were Davy lamps, with no glass round the gauze and later experiments proved that under these circumstances the flame from the lamp could be blown through the gauze and so ignite any gas that was there.

There was no doubt that there was a lot of gas. Turton gave evidence to the inquest that, when he got to Evans' and Clare's working place, about three weeks after the disaster, there was still gas coming from the face in large quantities and gas caused a great problem during the rescue operations.

As the last bodies were recovered. many who had been buried under large falls for about six weeks, the conditions in the mortuary were becoming intolerable. There was great pressure to get the bodies buried quickly and mistakes were made in identification of some bodies. There is also some doubt on the official number of victims. Henry Hall, Her Majesty's Inspector of Mines, stated the official figure of one hundred and eighty nine but references of the day and later research indicates that as many as two hundred and sixteen could have lost their lives.

Arthur Henry Lyne Evans.

Arthur Henry Lyne Evans.

Arthur Henry Lyne Evans, the compiler of the memorial album, was the eldest son of Josiah Evans and the grandson of Richard Evans. Richard Evans and his sons, Joseph and Josiah, had, since 1833 developed the Haydock Collieries into a very successful firm.

Arthur could be termed an outsider in the influential Evans family, embracing the Anglo-Catholic faith and taking no part in the running of the company. Throughout his life he was deeply involved in the Haydock community being a member of the Local Board, founding charities and societies and chairing many local meetings.

He lived at *The Homestead*, a large house in Church Road, Haydock and founded the Haydock Reading Room and Debating Society in 1884. It began as a Temperance Society but is now a popular local club, the *Reading Room*, being one of the last bastions of male chauvinism in the local community.

He was passionately involved in St. James the Great, Haydock, being a sacristan and supporting the church throughout his life. One of Arthur's greatest loves were the Passion Plays at Oberammergau, Germany and he gave many local lectures on the subject in aid of local charitable funds. St. James' still retain the fine wooden carvings he brought from Germany during his many visits.

Arthur Evans died, and is buried, in Oberammergau, after a tragic shooting accident. It is reputed that he committed suicide, but this has never been verified. In Oberammergau he is still remembered to the present day as he provided money for their church organ in the 1890's. His grave has recently been fitted with a new mahogany headpiece, showing the great regard that the local people still have for him.

S. James the Great in Haydock.

PHOTOGRAPHS FOR SALE.

I.   Exterior view of the Church, showing Lych Gate

II.   Ditto   ditto   from the S.E.........

III.   Sacristan preparing for Celebration ....

IV.   Verger extinguishing Candles ....

V.   Associate Sister in cap ....

VI.   Ditto   ditto   in bonnet and cloak...... ....

VII.   Banner Bearer..

1s. each; 6d. extra coloured.

VIII.   Group in Cassocks ....

IX.   Guild of S. Nicholas.................................

X.   Procession to Holy Baptism........................

XI.   Rev. Alan Greenwell in vestments, preceded by

        Server in tippet ....

1s. 6d. each; 6d. extra coloured.

May be had (by sending stamps and one for postage) from

Mr. ARTHUR EVANS, Haydock,

St. Helens.

Arthur as a photographer

Arthur Evans, photographer.

Among his many attributes, Arthur Evans was an accomplished Victorian photographer and many of the original photographs in this book are his work.

He had a photographic studio in a terraced house close to St. James Church, opposite Piele Road. The Unique record of the Wood Pit Disaster was made by Arthur for one his great friends, The Reverend Knox-Little of St. Albans, Manchester, another Anglo-Catholic church.

THE WOOD PIT, GENERAL VIEW.
Showing enginehouse and headgear at each shaft

The road to the pit.

On that fateful June morning in 1878, the men and boys who earned their living by winning coal from the Lower Florida Seam at the Wood Pit, Haydock, Lancashire, must have walked down this lane to their work. Little did they think that so many of them would feature on the list of victims that lost their lives in the explosion at the pit.

The Redford family, father and three sons, entered the cage. One of the boys realised that he had left his tea tin at home and hurried down the lane to get it. When he returned, the officials said that he was late for work and would not let him down the pit. His brother was killed in the explosion but his father was one of the survivors.

One hundred and eighty nine lives were lost on that fateful day and the disaster was the worst in the history of coal mining in Lancashire until the Pretoria Explosion, Hulton No.3, Westhoughton, in December, 1910, when three hundred and forty four lives were lost.

GENERAL VIEW OF WOOD PIT.
View of headgear and enginehouse. Downcast shaft.

General view of the Wood Pit.

The photograph shows the downcast shaft, tipplers and gantry. It was down this shaft that John Turton, the manager of the colliery, was lowered moments after the explosion. Fortunately the winding gear had not been damaged by the blast and rescue work could be started almost at once.

This is the original photograph that was reproduced as a postcard with an inscription that told of the date and place of the explosion. It was probably made and sold by Mr. Arthur Evans as there is a record that he offered his pictures for sale.

The damaged face.

Inscribed ' Peter Hughes'.

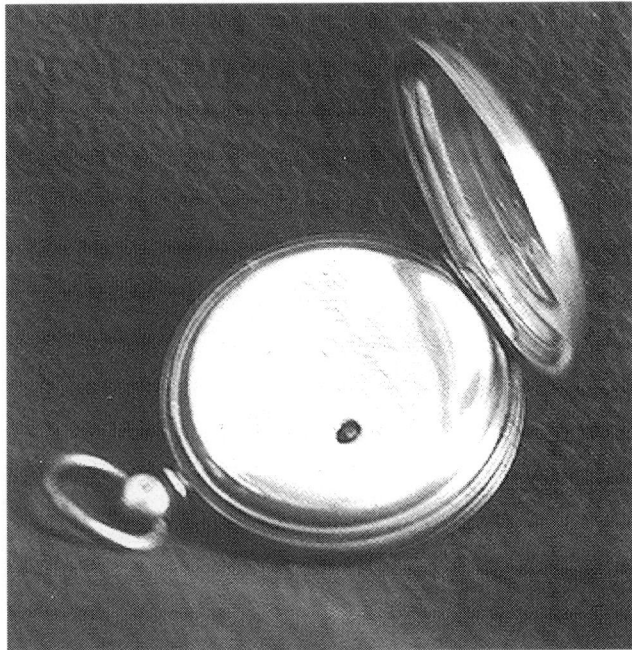

Time of the explosion.

From the official reports of the explosion we know that it occurred just before 11 a.m. There were about twenty three survivors of the blast. A unique record of the time of the disaster and the loss of some many lives, was preserved in Mr. Hughes' watch. He was one of the victims and the face was pierced by a fast moving stone to be stopped at the exact time of the explosion. The watch is cherished by the family as a unique record of how their great-grandfather lost his life.

Peter Hughes was a collier aged 37 years, of Old Whint Road, Haydock where he lived with his four children and wife, Alice, who identified his body

JOHN TURTON.
Certificated manager of the Wood Pit who risked his life by descending the downcast shaft immediately after the explosion thereby saving the lives of those who were brought up rescued from the poisonous effect of the afterdamp.

John Turton.

John Turton was a man born in Lodge Lane, Ashton and in 1878 lived at Brook House, Old Boston. He had worked all his life at the Wood Pit and risen to be manager of the colliery. He had no other mining experience except in that mine. This was a fact that was to emerge later when he was charged with not providing sufficient ventilation in the pit.

On the day of the explosion he had just come up the shaft after hearing the report of Roger Banks, the undermanager, and as he was walking away from the shaft he saw what all mining men dreaded, smoke and dust coming up the downcast shaft. Instinctively he knew that there had been an underground explosion. The cage was at the bottom of the shaft and the engineman, Arnold Shufflebotham, who had been winding wide coal, raised the cage. It was found to contain Matthew Chorley who was unconscious but alive and had managed to get into the cage at the shaft bottom. Chorley was the only survivor of the disaster to get out of the pit by his own efforts.

After sending for help, Turton told Shufflebotham to lower him down. The engineman was reluctant to do so but acceded to Turton's orders. At the bottom of the shaft, all was darkness and total confusion, but Turton knew it like the back of his hand. He opened and closed doors to make the best use of what little ventilation there was and went to look for the men. Those he found were unconscious from the afterdamp which filled the pit and he turned them on their faces so that they could breath what little fresh air there was. By his immediate efforts, at least twenty seven men owed their lives to John Turton that fateful day.

Her Majesty's Inspector of Mines for the District, Henry Hall, believed that the ventilation of the mine was faulty and that the Act had been breached. John Turton was summoned to face charges at Liverpool Stipendiary Magistrates Court, a summons that raised great anger in Haydock and prompted stormy protest meetings in the village. Turton's Managers Certificate was suspended but the case made no progress in court. One factor in his defence was that he had no experience of any other pit except Wood Pit where he had worked all his life and all charges against him were dropped.

His Certificate was restored and he finally retired from the service of Richard Evans and Company in the early years of this century. Had he not had the blemish of charges being made against him one can not help thinking that he may have been the only man to receive the Albert Medal for civilian bravery for his actions immediately after the explosion.

WOOD PIT, HAYDOCK.
Brow of the upcast shaft showing temporary arrangements for ventilation during extinction of furnace.

Steam into the Upcast Shaft from Two Locomotives.

Queen Victoria was very upset when she heard of the disaster and the Home Secretary, Mr. Cross, was instructed by Her to get news from Haydock. Mr Cross sent a telegraph to Mr. Hedley, Her Majesty's Inspector of Mines who was at the colliery, asking for details of the disaster and offering The Queens' sympathy to the relatives. The telegram was received the day of the disaster and from the reply that Mr. Hedley sent, it was clear that even at this early date, no one had any hope of anyone being found alive in the mine.

The rescue operations from the Saturday following the disaster were centred on the recovery of the bodies of the unfortunate men and boys. The main problem that confronted the rescue parties was that the mine was filled with firedamp. This posed several problems. first there was grave danger of a second explosion and second the men could not work in an atmosphere of gas. It was obvious that the gas had to be cleared in some way. The furnace had been extinguished after the disaster and several ways of improving the ventilation were considered.

Immediately after the disaster the men at the surface organised a bucket chain to pour cold water down the downcast shaft in an effort to clear the gas but it was soon clear that some other option would have to be used. The managers from other neighbouring collieries who had come to give help, the managers from Richard Evans and Company and the Mines Inspector held a meeting to see what could be done. It was thought a fan would be of use and steps were taken to get one from a Wigan colliery.

The use of steam jets was considered the most effectual and practical way to improve the ventilation and every boiler at the pit was used to provide steam for these.

They proved to be efficient but the problem was the quantity of steam that was required. The colliery boilers were not producing enough and every means at their disposal was used to make steam. The records of the time say that the colliery locomotives were used.

The photograph shows two Haydock Colliery locomotives, the Bellerophon and the Makerfield, making steam that is being piped from the steam release valve to the upcast, No.2 shaft.

Steam from the Bellerophon.

Steam from the Bellerophon.

When one of Arthur Evans' photographs was enlarged some interesting details emerged. A valve and pipe attached to the release valve of the locomotive, can be clearly seen. The pipe passes into a shed that was close to the upcast shaft. From here, the steam was passed down the shaft .

The locomotive is the *'Bellerophon'*, the only surviving Evans' locomotive and now running on the Keighley and Worth Valley Railway. Chalked on the locomotive is a piece of very good advice in the circumstances, *"No Smoking Allowed."*

THE UPCAST PIT HEAD

The Upcast Pit Head.

This very detailed photograph tells much of what was going on at the pit. The chains holding the cage in the shaft are visible and a spare cage next to the shaft has been prepared.

The wooden chimney on the left was probably something to do with the ventilation fan. As a result of a conference between the Inspectors and managers of R.E. & Co. and other local collieries, it was thought that a fan would be of use to clear the mine of gas. Mr. Barnes of the Atherton Collieries, who had been a former manager of the Wood Pit, went to Manchester to find a suitable fan. He was successful in procuring a Schiels fan and it was transported to Wigan but was not put to use at the colliery as the steam jets were found to be so successful in restoring the ventilation.

THE RE&CO. MANAGERS, 1874.

John Parkinson, James Potter, William Smethurst, John Houghton, John Turton, Henry Potter, Isaac Billinge,
James Twiss, John Fairhurst, John Chadwick, Thomas Litherland, Samuel Cook,
John Jackson, James Bain.

The R.E.&.Co. Managers, 1874.

At the time of the explosion, John Chadwick was the General Manger of all the Haydock Collieries. On the morning of the diaster he was at Pewfall Colliery and took charge of the operations when he arrived at the colliery.

Isaac Billinge had ben involved in the two explosions at Queen Pit, Haydock in 1868 and 1869 and was very lucky to escape with his life.

William Smethurst was involved with safety in the mines and conducted many experiments which were recognised nationally.

From;- *'Practical Mining Vol..5.'*

Ashworth's and Smethurst's experiments.

"In 1878 Mr. William Smethurst and the writer commenced experimenting with safety lamps, partly in consequence of their experience after the explosion at the Wood Pit, Haydock. They tested several types of lamps and communicated their results to the Manchester Geological Society, Vol. XV, March 25, 1879."

PREPARING REFRESHMENTS FOR THE EXPLORING PARTIES .

Refreshments for the Rescue Workers.

From the contemporary accounts of the disaster we know that the rescue parties came to the surface and were provided with refreshments. Just how they were dispensed is shown in this remarkable photographic record. The table is a pile of wooden blocks and the thickness of the bread that the man is cutting would have surely given sustenance to anyone who ate it.

The urn, that presumably was boiling water for tea, appears in the *'Illustrated London News'* report of the disaster when their artist must have visited the scene.

THE WOOD PIT, HAYDOCK.
Interior of Mortuary,
24th June, 1878.

The Mortuary.

This grim, sombre picture captures the stark horror of the disaster. The small memorial on the third of the seven coffins reads, *'George Whitley. Died 7th. June, 1878. Aged 20 years'*.

The bodies were taken by train from the pit head to the stable yard where a shed had been erected as a temporary mortuary. The relatives of the victims were admitted five at a time to identify their loved ones. The local papers of the time record harrowing and emotional scenes as the identifications were made. The coffins were made in the joiners shop at Richard Evans works and were reported to have been of the finest English oak provided at the Company's expense. Under the Law of the time the deceased had to appear before the Coroner's Court at the Ram's Head Inn for the official identification to be recorded.

IN MEMORY OF

THE UNFORTUNATE MINERS,

Killed by the Explosion at Wood Pit, June 7, 1878,

It is estimated that 204 have lost their lives by this awful Calamity, leaving 93 Widows and 282 Orphans.

Death did to them no warning give,
Therefore be careful how you live;
Begin in time, make no delay,
For no one knows their dying day.

Take warning by their sudden fall.,
Let you for death prepare;
For it will come ye know not when,
The manner, how or where.

Remembrance Cards.

The Remembrance Card was a popular Victorian custom and many survive to this day. One such card records that the disaster left ninety three widows and two hundred and eighty two orphaned children. Almost everyone in the village would have lost someone close to them.

There are many instances of a father and son appearing on the list of victims and some, like the Winstanley family, who lost a father and two sons. The father was the collier who won the coal from the face and he was employed by the Colliery Company. The collier had to pay his drawers himself. The drawers were responsible for loading the coal into tubs and transporting it from the face to the haulage and it was the custom for sons to act as drawers to their fathers.

ST. THOMAS GRAVEYARD, 1993.

St. Thomas' Churchyard, 1993.

In the early 1960's, the old part of the graveyard was in a very dilapidated state and required attention. Unlike many old churchyards where the stones were uprooted and placed round the site, the stones at St. Thomas' were laid flat over the grave and then the site was grassed over.

Many of the Wood pit victims were buried here. Recently, a researcher asked the permission of the Vicar to look for the victims graves and took rubbings of two, the Boon family and Thomas Wood. These graves and those of other victims can now be seen in the churchyard.

IN
MEMORY
OF
Catherine Wife of
Nathan Boon who died 24th
March 1877 Aged 42 Years.
Nathan Boon
Aged 45 Years.
Isaac their son
Aged 21 Years.
John their son
Aged 19 Years.
Thomas their son
Aged 18 Years.
William their son
Aged 16 Years.
Joseph their son
Aged 14 Years.
who lost their lives in the Wood
Pit Explosion June 7th 1878

The Boon Family Grave.

The Boon Family.

It was amazing to find that there are direct descendants of Nathan Boon alive today when Nathan and five of his sons featured in the list of the victims. There are several members of the family that are interested in their family tree and several have done detailed research. We are told by the family that Catherine, who was the mother of all the sons killed in the disaster, died in March, 1877, leaving Nathan with a large family. He married the widow of his next door neighbour soon after and before June, 1878.

There were three surviving children. One left school at the age of fourteen the day of the disaster and was due to start work at the pit the following Monday. The three surviving boys were taken in by an Aunt and brought up in the Leigh area.

*Two gravestones in St.Oswald's,
Ashton-in-Makerfield.*

Two Gravestones in St. Oswald's Graveyard.

There are but three gravestones standing that bear the names of the victims and none of them say how they died. They are in St. Oswald's churchyard and Canon Ripley, who has served the Parish for many years, informed us that was 'the poor part of the graveyard'.

Another piece was added to the story when a great grandchild of James Greenall, one of the victims, contacted the authors when she was researching her family history. She knew that her grandfather had been killed in the disaster and had a very old photograph of his gravestone. From other records, we knew that he was buried in St. Oswald's churchyard and as soon as we saw the old photograph we knew that he was next to Thomas Thompson. The clue came from the shape of the stone on the right of the grave. We were also sent a copy of James Greenall's death certificate.

Thomas Thompson lived in Lodge Lane, Haydock and left a widow, Eliza. John Wilton was a collier of Sumner's Yard, Ashton-in-Makerfield who left a wife and five children. His name does not appear in the official list of victims but is included in many local accounts and lists of the disaster.

In Affectionate Remembrance

CERTIFIED COPY OF AN ENTRY OF DEATH

GIVEN AT THE GENERAL REGISTER OFFICE, LONDON

Application Number _289385_

REGISTRATION DISTRICT	_Warrington_							
_1878_ DEATH in the sub-district of _Newton-in-Makerfield_ in the _County of Lancaster_								
Columns:— 1	2	3	4	5	6	7	8	9
No.	When and Where died	Name and surname	Sex	Age	Occupation	Cause of death	Signature, description and residence of informant	When registered	Signature of registrar
61	_Eighth June 1878 Wood Pits Haydock_	_James Greenall_	_Male_	_34 Years_	_Coal miner of Haydock_	_Injuries to back, etc. Higher Florida Mine sudden issue Found dead_	_Certificate received from J.E. Driffield Coroner for Lancashire Inquest held thirteenth July 1878_	_Sixteenth July 1878_	_[signature] Registrar_

CERTIFIED to be a true copy of an entry in the certified copy of a Register of Deaths in the District above mentioned.
Given at the GENERAL REGISTER OFFICE, LONDON, under the Seal of the said Office, the _18th_ day of _November_ 19_81_.

DX 395443

This certificate is issued in pursuance of the Births and Deaths Registration Act 1953. Section 34 provides that any certified copy of an entry purporting to be sealed or stamped with the seal of the General Register Office shall be received as evidence of the birth or death to which it relates without any further or other proof of the entry, and no certified copy purporting to have been given in the said Office shall be of any force or effect unless it is sealed or stamped as aforesaid.

CAUTION:—It is an offence to falsify a certificate or to make or knowingly use a false certificate or a copy of a false certificate intending it to be accepted as genuine to the prejudice of any person, or to possess a certificate knowing it to be false without lawful authority.

Form A504M Dd 8098253 7640180 20st 8/87 Mcr(734596)

James Greenall's Death Certificate.

40

James Greenall's Death Certificate.

The certificate reads;-

REGISTRATION DISTRICT. Warrington.

1878 DEATH in the sub-district of Newton in Makerfield in the County of Lancaster.

No. 361.

When and where died. Seventh June 1878 Wood Pits Haydock.

Name and surname. James Greenall

Sex Male

Age 34 years.

Occupation Coalminer of Kenyons Lane Haydock.

Cause of death Explosion of firedamp in Higher Florida Mine Sudden outburst. Found dead.

Signature, description and residence of informant. Certificate received from C.E. Driffield, Coroner, July 1878.

When registered. Thirty first August 1878.

Signature of registrar. George Upperton, Registrar.

In
Memory of
EDWARD EVANS.
WHO DIED JUNE 7TH 1878.
AGED 40 YEARS.

ALSO ROBERT EVANS.
WHO DIED JUNE 7TH 1878.
AGED 19 YEARS.

In
Memory of
JOHN EVANS.
WHO DIED JUNE 7TH 1878
AGED 17 YEARS.

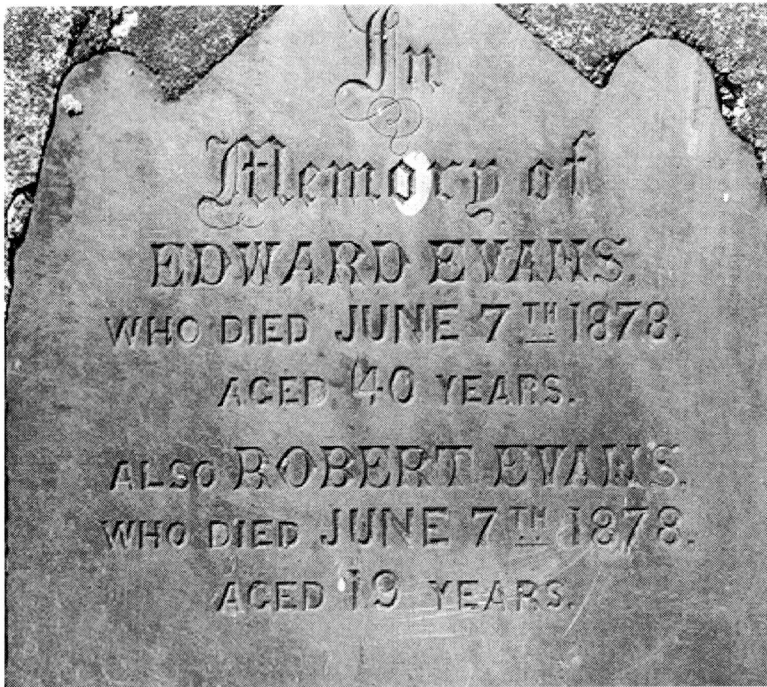

Gravestones at Wargrave.

The Evans Family.

Edward Evans was the father of John and Robert. Edward was a collier and the two sons worked as drawers. The family lived in Viaduct Street, Earlestown and their mother, Sarah, indentified the bodies.

John's body was recovered in the early rescue operations and buried on the 11th. June. Sarah had to wait until her husband and other son were recovered. They were buried under falls and were buried at Wargrave on the 23rd. June.

IN MEMORY OF

EDWARD MANLEY
OF MOLD.
WHO DIED JUNE 7, 1878,
AGED 21.
SAFE IN THE ARMS OF JESUS.

In

Affectionate Remembrance of
GEORGE EVANS, WHO DIED
JUNE 7TH 1878, AGED 29 YEARS,
ALSO JOHN WILLIAMS,
WHO DIED JUNE 7TH 1878,
AGED 28 YEARS.
Farewell dear wife, my life is past,
Faithful I loved you to the last,
And on my children pray pity take
And love them for their father's sake.

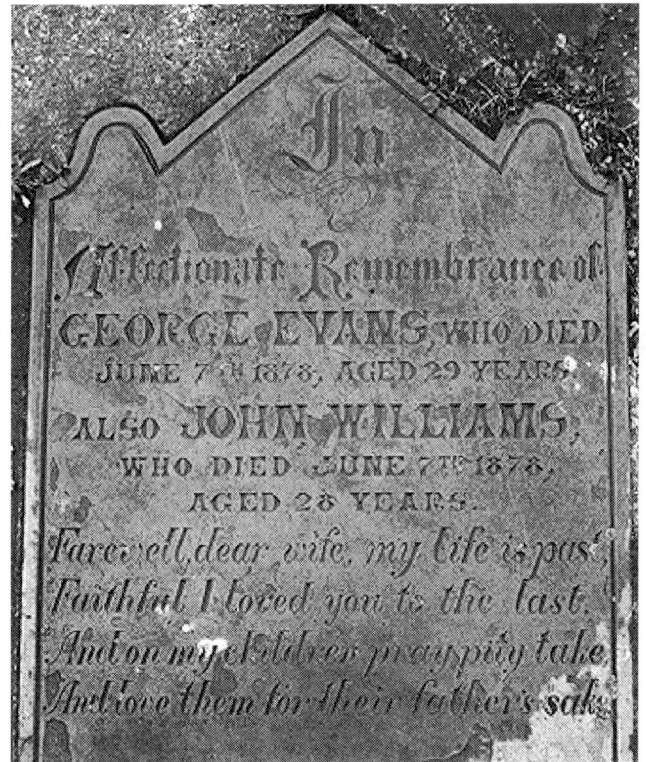

More Gravestones at Wargrave.

George Evans and John Williams.

There were many Welshmen working in the Lancashire coalfield at the time. There had been a bitter dispute in the North Wales coalfield some years earlier and many had walked to Lancashire find work. They found employment in the Haydock Collieries and local families were glad to have a lodger to supplement the family income.

Edward Manley of Mold aged 21 years was one of these men. Many worked as drawers and were known only by their nicknames like '*Canary*' and '*Taff*' which gave rise to problems of identification at the inquest. Many of the Welsh victims were taken by rail on a special train from Haydock Station to Mold where they were buried in their native country.

George Evans was a collier who lived at 29, Viaduct Street, Earlestown. He left a wife and four children. John Williams was a collier who lived in Booth Street, Earlestown who left a wife and three children. His wife, Jane, identified him from his clothing.

ST. JAMES THE GREAT,
HAYDOCK.

St. James' Church, Haydock.

The church of St. James the Great, Haydock, featured in ecclesiastical history. It was one of the first Anglo-catholic churches in the country springing from the Oxford Movement of the mid nineteenth century

The Oxford Movement was revolutionary religious movement within the Anglican Church. It was initiated by a group of graduates at Oxford and created a completely different aspect of the established Church that still survives to the present day. Their controversial idea was to reform the Church of England and make it more catholic in form and appearance. The Movement was also known as the Catholic Revival. The movement swept the country in the later half of the 19th. century and became known for its elaborate rituals and ceremonies. Various ministers were imprisoned and church-goers were vilified and treated with scorn by Anglicans throughout Victorian times. However, the movement did gain a foothold in the country due to the dedication of its ministers and followers. St. Albans, Manchester was in the forefront of the movement.

INTERIOR OF ST. JAMES. THE GREAT.
WHITSUNTIDE, 1878.

The Interior of St. James' Church, Haydock.

There were strong connections between St. Albans, Manchester and St. James the Great, Haydock as they were sister churches in the Catholic Revival, both being accused of ritualism and Popery during their history. It is ironic that when the Haydock Parish was divided later in the century, the new chapel was named St. Albans but when it was demolished and a new church built, it took the name St. Mark's, creating the well known local animosity between the two churches.

Another amusing parallel between the two churches was 'The Pig's Head Case' at St. James' and the 'Donkey Ride' at St. Albans. In 1868 the 'Pig's Head Case' raised such a storm in the ecclesiastical world, that Haydock became the talk of the country.

The Vicar, Alan Greenwell, was accused of offering a pig's head up to the altar during a Harvest Festival. The resulting commotion was reported in many newspapers and appeared in *'The Illustrated London News'*.

At St. Albans, Reverend Knox-Little was accused of riding a donkey round the church, as if he was Christ. These alarming occurrences and the resulting furore mat appear trivial today but they were taken very seriously in the nineteenth century.

The church was to witness the funerals of twenty six of the victims and heard a very emotional sermon from the Reverend Sherlock on the Sunday after the disaster which was a Whit Sunday.

ST. JAMES' GRAVEYARD,
June, 1878.

St. James' Graveyard.

This view of the graveyard must have been taken after the graves of the victims had just been filled. It was reported that Vicar Sherlock had to fight hard to control his emotions as be read the burial service for many of his flock. The Colliery Brass Band played the '*Dead March*' from '*Saul*' and as a member of the band was lowered into his grave one of the bandsman came forward and placed the dead man's cornet on the coffin to be buried with him. The photograph captures the utter desolation that must have been felt of the widows, orphans, sons, brothers and sisters of the victims in Haydock in the Summer of 1878.

S. JAMES ✝ THE GREAT,

HAYDOCK.

"When our heads are bowed with woe,
When our bitter tears o'erflow
When we mourn the lost, the dear,
Jesu, Son of Mary, hear!"

ON

SUNDAY, JUNE 30, 1878,

(2ND SUNDAY AFTER TRINITY.)

The OFFERTORIES at all the SERVICES will be devoted to the RELIEF FUND for the Widows and Orphans rendered destitute by the Wood Pit Explosion.

THE SERVICES WILL BE:---

8.0 a.m.---Holy Communion.

10.30 a.m.---Mattins.

11.15 a.m.---Holy Communion and Sermon.

3.0 p.m.---Evensong and Sermon.

7.0 p.m.---Litany and Sermon.

The Preacher at 11.15 a.m., 3.0 and 7.0 p.m. will be the

REV.

W. J. KNOX LITTLE, M.A.

Rector of S. Alban's, Manchester.

"Bear ye one another's burdens, and so fulfil the law of Christ."

Poster for services,
30th. June, 1878.

The Memorial Service.

On Sunday 30th. June following the disaster, a memorial service for the victims was held at St. James Church. The poster was displayed to inform people of the event when the Reverend Knox-Little, Vicar of St. Albans, Manchester, came to preach at the service. Knox-Little had become well known in the Manchester district due to the power of his preaching and the strength of his religious conviction.

He had been at St. Albans since 1875 and moved to a new living at Hoar Cross, Staffordshire. He was living in Staffordshire when, in 1881, he was made a Canon of Worcester Cathedral. When he retired in 1907, he went to live in Worcester.

The album contains a poem by Dora Greenwell. Many people im mining areas were moved to put pen to paper and express their thoughts in verse after a disaster. These poems were generally not of a high literary standard but record the emotion of the events. However, these lines were written by a distinguished writer of the times who had several books of verse published.

THE WOMEN OF HAYDOCK.

"In Rama was there a voice heard, lamentation and bitter weeping; Rachel weeping for her children and would not be comforted, because they were not." - Book of the Prophet Jeremiah.

Come Summer, come Winter, come shine, come rain,
There's not one of them will come back again.
They went, as they'd gone so often before,
And we'll never see them any more.

We were all of us busy, and some were baking,
'And some were tydying up and making
All ready for dinner; the babes were sleeping
Warm in their cots, and the children keeping
All the whole street at rack and riot,
When all in the house was peace and quiet,
Till some of us went to our doors and were saying,
"Come Bairns, it's time to give over playing."
And not a word the children were minding,
Such joy in their pastime they were finding,
When, all at once, it came like a stroke,
And our hearts in a moment's time were broke!
The little street's as still as stone,
And there isn't a sound if it isn't a groan,
Or a sob, or a wife's or a mother's cry
That had lost "the apple of her eye."

Oh, mothers, daughters, sweethearts, and wives,
The joy and the pride's taken out of our lives,
It's our one and our all that we've lost today!
Oh, children, you've got no more need to play,
Or to teaze your mammy's to let you sit up
At nights for a sip out of daddy's cup.
Ye may go to bed soon, ye may go to bed late,
You'll steal no more bits from off daddy's plate,
For you've got no daddies now, no Brothers;
You may sit down besides your poor Mothers.
For be it the day-shift or be it the night,
There's and end of the footstep that made it all right.
Here's a cap and a jacket, and in the chest
We've got safe put their Sunday best.
And their song-books and Hymn-books are on the shelves,
And all that was theirs except themselves;
And all looks just as it used before,
But we'll never see them anymore.

And the sun will shine on their graves, and the rain
Will beat, and the harvest will come again,
And the children will play before the door,
And all will go on as it did before,
But we'll never see them anymore.

Dora Greenwell.

Dora was born at Greenwell Ford, near Lanchester in County Durham. Her father was William Thomas Greenwell, a country squire and Justice of the Peach who became Deputy Lieutenant for County Durham. Her brother, the Rev Alan Greenwell was appointed the Rector of Golborne when the church was built in 1849. Alan was also the first Vicar of Haydock. The church was then called St. Aidan's.

Dora came to the area with her brother, father and mother and remained in the area for four years. The parish was described as '*a parish carved out of a neglected district*' and Dora helped her brother in his duties. The family stayed in the area for only four years when they returned to their native Durham due to the failing health of their father.

Miss Greenwell published her first volume of poems in 1848 and a second edition appeared in 1850 so one edition was published during her stay in the area. According to her biographers;-

> "It was here that she rubbed off her shyness among the brusque independent people and acquired her pleasant manner with the poor, poor not only in material things but in health and friendliness. The unattractive beings hidden away, here and there, which anyone may find by looking for them".

Dora was described as 'tall, very slender, with a gentle hesitating manner and soft cooing voice. A rather slim, dark woman of elegant, serious type with a particularly pleasing voice and mode of elocution. and such eyes; not black either, but dark, luminous brown eyes and wonderfully vivacious.'

After the family returned to Durham, it is most likely that she kept in touch with friends that she had made in the district, particularly those associated with the churches in Golborne and Haydock. When she heard of the Wood Pit Explosion she put pen to paper and sent the poem to Arthur Evans, who included it in the commemorative album for the Rev. Knox-Little.

The

Haydock Colliery

Explosion

Relief Fund.

Collection for the Relief Fund.

Collecting for the Relief Fund.

There were collections and events organised all over the district and further afield to collect money for the Haydock Explosion Fund. The tossing of coins into a blanket was a common method to make a collection but it obviously required the close supervision of a policeman. If this was the Haydock 'bobby' then it will be Sergeant Gardiner who was stationed at Haydock and was the sole officer to look after a silent stunned crowd of about a thousand at the pit head on the day of the disaster. An engraving of the scene in the photograph appeared in the *'Illustrated London News'*.

The Haydock Colliery Explosion Relief Fund.

A Committee was quickly set up to make provision to institute a Relief Fund for the widows and orphans left by the disaster under the chairmanship of Lord Derby. Contributions came in from all over the country and Queen Victoria donated £100.

Details of the donations appeared periodically in the local newspapers of the day and a final total of over £25,000 was raised. In a recent cataloguing session at the St. Helens Local History Library and Archive a document came to light. It was a proof copy recording the donations that made up the full £25,000. The *'Introductory Note'* gives details of what the beneficiaries of the Fund received and the conditions under which they were paid.

It is of interest to see where the contributions came from. Many communities in other coalfields of the county who had been visited by disaster were only too pleased to give to the Fund. There were such donations from the Bardsley Colliery Accident and Funeral Society, Ashton-under-Lyne, Altham collieries, Accrington and The Workpeople at Leycott (Leycette) Colliery, Newcastle, Staffordshire.

The attention of the Victorian public was focused on the events in Haydock by articles in the *'Illustrated London News'* and reports in national newspapers.

THE

HAYDOCK COLLIERY

EXPLOSION RELIEF FUND.

List of Subscriptions

RECEIVED BY THE

EXECUTIVE COMMITTEE.

WIGAN :

WALL, PRINTER, "OBSERVER" OFFICE, WALLGATE.

1879.

INTRODUCTORY NOTE.

APPENDED is a Cash Statement, and a List of Subscriptions received up to March 31st, 1879, by the Executive Committee of the Haydock Relief Fund, at Parr's Bank, Warrington, and not passed through the several accounts kindly opened by the chief magistrates of many cities and towns.

The number of deaths caused by the explosion was 189; there were 88 widows to be provided for, and at the time of the disaster, 205 children. Nineteen children have since been born; one has died, and there are at present on the fund 223. Three of the widows have died, two have re-married, and there remain 83 in receipt of relief.

The scales of relief adopted are those of the Lancashire and Cheshire Miners' Permanent Relief Society, viz. :—5s. per week for each widow, and 2s. 6d. per week for each child—boys until they are 12, and girls until they are 13. Under the rules of the Colliery Club, the widows were entitled to 5s. weekly and the children 1s. weekly, for three months; and during this period these payments were supplemented by grants from the fund sufficient to bring the relief to the children up to 2s. 6d. per week.

Before deciding upon the method of administering the fund, the Executive Committee caused inquiries to be made as to the manner in which the Hartley, Blantyre, and other large funds are being distributed, and they have adopted a system which has hitherto worked very smoothly and satisfactorily.

The accident occurred shortly after there had been a considerable drain upon public charity by reason of the Blantyre disaster; and at too long an interval before the Abercarn and Princess Alice accidents to partake of the great flow of generosity which those calamities called forth. The funds raised to deal with the distress occasioned by these three accidents were all considerably larger than that subscribed for Haydock, and they were probably obtained with much less difficulty.

GEORGE L. CAMPBELL,

SECRETARY.

Magistrates' Room, Newton-le-Willows.

List of Subscriptions.

	£	s.	d.
HER MAJESTY THE QUEEN	100	0	0
Liverpool Subscriptions	3260	16	6
R. Evans and Co....	3000	0	0
Manchester Subscriptions...	1468	3	0
Mansion House Subscriptions	1061	1	6
Salford Subscriptions	686	4	1
Workpeople of R. Evans and Co.	630	8	2

Collections made in the Catholic Churches of the Diocese of Liverpool.

	£	s.	d.
The Bishop of Liverpool ...	10	0	0
Liverpool, St. Nicholas', pro Cathedral	7	17	10
All Souls'...	1	6	6
St. Anne's	2	18	6
St. Alphonsus'	4	0	0
St. Anthony's	6	0	0
St. Augustine's	3	15	3
St. Bridget's	23	0	0
St. Francis Xavier's	16	8	6
Holy Cross	1	17	6
St. John's...	5	0	0
St. Joseph's	1	10	0
St. Michael's	15	0	0
St. Philip Neri's	6	15	0
Our Lady Immaculate	4	0	8
,, of Mercy	1	3	6
,, of Reconciliation ...	4	10	0

				£	s.	d.
St. Patrick's	...	...	...	15	6	0
St. Peter's	...	...	...	13	7	0
St. Sylvester's	...	...	...	2	17	6
St. Vincent's	...	...	...	4	0	0
St. Sepulchre's—Ford	...	...	2	2	0
Aigburth	...	...	...	2	18	10
Anderton	...	...	...	1	14	0
Appleton	...	...	...	6	11	0
Ashton...	...	...	...	17	10	0
Rev. G. O'Reilly...	...	...	5	0	0
Aughton	...	...	...	6	8	0
Bedford Leigh...	...	...	...	3	17	0
Birchley	...	...	...	5	1	6
Birkdale	...	...	...	13	0	0
Bishop Eton	...	...	...	0	5	6
Blackbrook	...	...	...	3	6	0
Blackpool	...	...	...	2	0	0
Bolton-le-Sands	...	...	...	7	6	0
Bootle, St. Alexander's	...	...	5	3	0
St. James's	...	...	...	9	4	6
Burscough	...	...	...	9	1	0
Catforth	...	...	...	0	7	6
Chorley, Sacred Heart	...	...	2	2	6
Claughton	...	...	...	6	0	0
Clayton Green...	...	...	...	5	9	2
Coniston	...	...	...	0	6	0
Cottam...	...	...	...	4	0	0
Croft	...	...	...	3	12	6
Fernyhalgh	...	...	...	4	2	6
Fleetwood	...	...	...	0	9	6
Formby	...	...	...	9	6	0
Garstang	...	...	...	6	13	5
Rev. J. Hennessy	...	...	0	10	0
Gillmoss	...	...	...	3	11	0
Golborne	...	...	...	4	0	0
Goosenargh	...	...	...	1	15	0

	£	s.	d.
Great Crosby	6	10	0
Great Eccleston	3	2	6
Hindley	3	0	0
Hornby	1	0	0
Rev. G. Fisher	1	0	0
Huyton	3	3	0
Ince	2	6	0
Ince-Blundell	8	0	0
Lancaster	15	0	0
Lea	3	11	0
Leyland	2	2	0
Little Crosby	8	8	0
Lydiate	3	17	6
Lytham	10	7	0
Mawdesley	3	0	0
Netherton	1	17	0
Newsham	1	10	6
Old Swan	8	15	0
Ormskirk	8	15	0
Orrell	4	4	6
Peasley Cross	3	2	0
Pemberton	4	5	0
Portico...	5	10	0
Prescot...	2	2	0
Preston, St. Ignatius	1	0	0
St. Wilfrid's	9	0	0
St. Walburga's	2	7	2
Rainford	2	0	0
Rainhill (2nd instalment)	3	14	0
Rixton...	0	8	4
Scarisbrick	4	2	6
Skelmersdale	2	3	0
South Hill	4	2	10
Standish	4	6	6
St. Helens, Sacred Heart	3	0	0
Sutton...	7	17	6

	£ s. d.	£ s. d.
Thurnham	4 10 6	
Tyldesley	4 13 0	
Ulverston	2 10 0	
Walton-on-the-Hill	3 4 0	
Warrington, St. Albans	3 5 6	
St. Mary's	2 13 2	
Waterloo	4 19 5	
Weld Bank	5 0 0	
Widnes	6 17 0	
Wigan, St. John's	9 15 6	
St. Mary's	7 10 1	
St. Patrick's	4 0 0	
Willows	3 17 0	
Woolston	2 0 0	
Woolton Much	4 8 5	
Yealand	3 11 8	
Isle of Man, Douglas...	1 19 4	
Ramsay	0 14 0	
		537 5 7
W. J. Legh, M.P.		500 0 0
Warrington Subscriptions		428 18 1
Chester Subscriptions		393 12 10
Widnes Subscriptions		344 19 3
Simpson's Bowl		575 7 8
Halifax Subscriptions		250 0 0
Oldham Subscriptions		241 10 8
Lord Gerard		200 0 0
Hindley Green Explosion Fund (Bolton Subscription)		200 0 0
Bootle Borough Subscriptions		161 14 8
Bolton Subscriptions		110 0 0
Gateshead Subscriptions		107 10 6
The Earl of Derby		105 0 0
Hugh Mason		105 0 0
The Duke of Westminster		100 0 0
The Earl of Crawford and Balcarres		100 0 0

	£	s.	d.
The High Sheriff of Lancashire (N. Eckersley)...	100	0	0
Miss Lydia Evans (The Heyes)	100	0	0
J. Hadfield Evans	100	0	0
Miss E. H. Evans...	100	0	0
Miss Alice Evans	100	0	0
Miss Kate Evans	100	0	0
T. W. Legh	100	0	0
Clifton and Kersley Coal Co.	98	12	8
St. James's Church, Haydock	97	7	1
Ridding's Collieries	73	4	2
Chorley Subscriptions	63	17	8
Collected in Sheets at the Pits	63	6	8
Grove Chapel, Camberwell, London	63	0	0
Winwick Parish	58	17	10
Locomotive Works, Crewe	58	0	0
St. Peter's, Newton	55	2	6
North Shore Mills Company	52	10	0
Stephenson Clarke and Co.	52	10	0
Emmanuel Church, Earlestown	53	0	0
Employés of the L. and N. W. Railway Company (Waggon Department, Earlestown) ...	52	0	10
Wigan Concerts	50	2	0
Harding and Parrington	50	0	0
John Mercer	50	0	0
Sullivan and Company, Limited	50	0	0
John Pearson	50	0	0
J. F. Hodges	50	0	0
James Bland and Co.	50	0	0
Hird, Dawson, and Hardy	50	0	0
J. Harvie	50	0	0
A. Knowles and Son	50	0	0
Geo. McCorquodale	50	0	0
T. Comber	50	0	0
John Chadwick	50	0	0
Roger Leigh	50	0	0
Norley Coal Company	50	0	0

	£	s.	d.
White Moss Coal Company	50	0	0
Jas. Latham	50	0	0
Joseph Butler and Company	50	0	0
James Stott and Co.	50	0	0
Lieutenant-Colonel Steble	50	0	0
F. S. Powell (half subscription)	50	0	0
Offertory, Ormskirk Parish Church	50	0	0
Thomas Whiffin	50	0	0
W. Ramsden	50	0	0
E. Pilkington	50	0	0
A. Pilkington	50	0	0
Cork Steamship Company	50	0	0
Widnes Collections	48	12	1
Collected at St. Mary's, Windermere	43	10	3
Bowdon Parish Church	40	3	7
Walmsley Chapel Collection	36	15	3
Pratt and Ellis	33	1	6
St. John's Church, Altrincham	31	0	0
Lord Winmarleigh	30	0	0
Hyde and Houghton Coal Co.	30	0	0
Workmen at Riding Lane, Mains, and Bam- furlong Collieries	29	13	9
Employés of Ackers, Whitley, and Co.	28	4	0
St. Thomas's Church, Ashton	27	2	2
St. Stephen's Church, Astley	26	11	0
Rev. Christopher Prescot...	26	10	0
Crow Lane Chapel	25	9	8
Sir Thomas B. Birch	25	0	0
Buxton Independent Chapel	25	0	0
Ellis Lever...	25	0	0
Lieut.-Colonel Blundell	25	0	0
Richard Walmesley	25	0	0
Chapel Street Congregational Chapel, Southport	25	0	0
Clayton and Brooke	25	0	0
A. B. Forwood	25	0	0
The Bishop of Chester	25	0	0

	£	s.	d.
Macfie and Sons	25	0	0
Mrs. Oliver Heywood	25	0	0
Lord Skelmersdale	25	0	0
J. Brewis	25	0	0
Bradford Colliery Co.	25	0	0
R. Pennington, sen.	25	0	0
Altrincham Gas Co.	25	0	0
Catholic Churches, Newton	25	0	0
E. Bird Foster	35	0	0
C. F. Foster	25	0	0
G. E. Foster	25	0	0
C. Pilkington	25	0	0
G. C. Dobell	25	0	0
John Johnson and Sons	25	0	0
G. Hargreaves and Co., Newchurch	25	0	0
T. Stone and Son	25	0	0
William Crompton	25	0	0
Chamber Colliery Co., Limited	25	0	0
Whitecross Co.	25	0	0
Rhyl Commissioners	24	3	7
Workpeople of W. Ramsden, Shackerley Colliery, Tyldesley	24	0	0
Wesleyan Chapels, Bold Street and Bewsey Road, Warrington	28	13	9
Crow Lane Chapel Collection	25	9	8
Bradford Colliery Company	25	0	0
St. Ann's Church, Sale	23	10	11
Clare and Ridgway	22	10	0
All Saints' Church, Wigan	22	6	10
Billinge Church	21	3	6
Workpeople, Annesley Colliery, Nottingham ...	21	2	2
Rev. Thomas Blackburne...	21	0	0
Makerfield Minstrels	21	0	0
St. Chrysostom's Church, Liverpool (per T. Brakell)	20	12	4
Pym Williamson	20	10	0

	£	s.	d.
Hope Chapel, Wigan	20	8	0
William Cliff	20	0	0
The Bishop of Manchester	20	0	0
A Friend (per Bishop of Manchester	20	0	0
T. J. Gillespie	20	0	0
Walter Mayhew	20	0	0
Rev. J. Whitley	20	0	0
Edward Scott	20	0	0
John Thomson, Sankey Hill	20	0	0
Henry Burrows	20	0	0
Robert Forward	20	0	0
J. Ireland Blackburne, M.P.	20	0	0
The Mayor of Bradford	20	0	0
T. B. Crosse	20	0	0
Wilson and Co., Liverpool	20	0	0
Right Hon. R. A. Cross, M.P.	20	0	0
J. H. Birley	20	0	0
Walter Thomson	20	0	0
Poynton and Worth Collieries' Accident Society, Stockport	20	0	0
Altham Colliery Company	20	0	0
P. O'Brian...	20	0	0
Workpeople of Crow Orchard Company, Limited	20	0	0
P. Stubs	20	0	0
Herbert Ainsworth	20	0	0
Wigan Royal Albert Amateur Minstrels ...	20	0	0
Workpeople of Wingate Grange Colliery ...	20	0	0
Dewhurst and Berry, Skelmersdale	20	0	0
Officials, &c., Blackwell Colliery	20	0	0
Thompson and Co....	20	0	0
Thomas May	20	0	0
Miners at Astley Deep Pit	19	14	0
De Castro's "Theatre of Varieties," Leigh ...	18	18	2
Entertainment, Carter-street, London	18	11	6
Workpeople, Bestwood Colliery, near Nottingham	18	5	2
Employés of J. Diggle, Westleigh Collieries ...	18	2	6

	£	s.	d.
St. George's Church, Altrincham...	18	1	0
Harvest Thanksgiving, St. John's Church, Lancaster	17	5	7
Pelton Fell Colliery, Chester-le-street	17	3	6
Employés, Messrs. Rylands, Wigan :—			
Colliery 3 5 0			
Spinning Department 4 7 6			
Weaving 9 11 4			
	17	3	10
Parish Church, Davenham	17	0	0
Barrow Hematite Steel Co., Dalton-in-Furness ...	16	16	0
St. Joseph's, Wrightington	16	14	0
Parish Church, Warrington	16	9	4
St. Mary's, Arley Hall	16	4	6
Employés, Wigan and Whiston Coal Co. :—			
Platt Lane Colliery 3 9 6			
Whiston Colliery... ... ... 7 0 10			
Prescot 5 3 0			
	15	13	4
McCorquodale and Co.'s Employés	15	19	1
Wesleyan Methodist Chapel, Leigh	15	3	0
Employés of T. & R. Stone, Wigan Junction Railway	15	17	6
All Saints' Parish Church, Hindley	15	2	6
Rev. T. H. France, Hayhurst	15	0	0
Old Parish Church, Chorley	15	0	0
Church of the Holy Innocents, Liverpool ...	15	0	0
All Saints', Elton-in-Bury	14	8	5
Leigh Parish Church	14	8	2
Wesleyan Chapel, Earlestown	14	10	0
Wesleyan Chapel, Haydock	14	6	8
Dalton Church Collection...	14	6	2
Workmen, R. Evans's Salt Works	13	13	7
Workpeople Tinby Colliery, near Nottingham ...	13	11	7
Congregational Church, Leigh	13	8	2
Workpeople Liverpool United Gaslight Company	13	11	10
Servants, Workmen, &c., Haydock Lodge Asylum	13	3	1
St. James's, Rusholme	13	0	2
Workpeople Tanfield Collieries, Durham ...	12	14	6

	£	s.	d.
Upholland Church	12	14	2
Kirkby Roman Catholic Church...	12	13	2
Pennington Church	12	10	9
Workpeople Denton and Haughton Collieries ...	12	10	0
Joseph Evans	12	10	0
Christ Church, Timperley	12	10	0
Half Harvest Thanksgiving, S. Paul's, Chester...	12	8	6
Collection, Bethel Chapel, Bury	12	5	0
Workpeople, Picksley, Sims, and Co., Leigh ...	12	4	9
Pemberton Parish Church	12	0	6
Workpeople, Taversall Collieries...	12	0	0
Workpeople Rosebridge Colliery Company ...	11	16	1
Henry Brown	11	12	0
Congregational Church, Ashton-in-Makerfield ...	11	10	10
St. Thomas's Church, Golborne	11	10	2
Workpeople, Bridgewater Trustees, Colliery ...	11	5	2
Hartford Church	11	4	5
Employés Bradford Colliery	11	13	6
Workpeople, Chamber Colliery, Hollinwood ...	11	2	3
Workpeople, Stonehill Colliery, Farnworth ...	11	1	6
Baptist Chapel, Haydock...	11	1	0
Rev. W. Ogden, Vicar, Churchwardens, and Congregation of St. Peter's Church, Ashton-under-Lyne	11	0	4
Borrow and Co., Newton...	10	19	0
Nook Pits	10	17	3
St. Paul's Congregational Chapel, Wigan ...	10	13	6
Lee, Houseman, and Brodie	10	10	0
Derby Bowling Club, Liverpool	10	10	0
Turton and Sons	10	10	0
Kneeshaw, Lupton, and Co.	10	10	0
C. Borrow and Co., Earlestown	10	10	0
Grand Clothing Hall Co., Warrington	10	10	0
Chester Gas Co.	10	10	0
Bishop of St Albans	10	10	0
J. L. Hedley	10	10	0

	£	s.	d.
Jos. Pease and Co.	10	10	0
Friends at Pontlotgn, Cardiff	10	10	0
H. Frank	10	10	0
Workpeople, Bradley Colliery, Standish... ...	10	7	6
Bickerstaffe Church	10	0	3
The Mayor of Manchester	10	0	0
Bancroft and Co.	10	0	0
G. Hadfield, jun.	10	0	0
W. Beamont	10	0	0
Rev. H. Sherlock	10	0	0
W. S. & W. Caine...	10	0	0
G. T. McCorquodale	10	0	0
Howard and Co.	10	0	0
J. Massey	10	0	0
T. Wadehouse	10	0	0
Hon. A. Egerton, M.P.	10	0	0
A. Hewlett	10	0	0
J. M. L.	10	0	0
Whitley and Co.	10	0	0
Roscoe and Lord	10	0	0
Tyldesley Colliery, Tyldesley, near Manchester...	10	0	0
St. George's Church, Wigan	10	0	0
Black Park Colliery, Ruabon	10	0	0
Workpeople, Garswood Coal and Iron Company,			
Limited	10	0	0
Richard Newsham	10	0	0
W. Park and Co.	10	0	0
Thomas Molyneux	10	0	0
Evans Bros.	10	0	0
Medley and Son	10	0	0
J. Thomas	10	0	0
P. B. Drinkwater	10	0	0
Thomas Ellames Withington	10	0	0
James Nicholson	10	0	0
R. Hampson, Bowdon	10	0	0
J. and W. Waddington	10	0	0

	£	s.	d.
J. E. Pardey	10	0	0
Workpeople, Brewis and Co.	10	0	0
R. Pennington, jun.	10	0	0
W. F. Gooch	10	0	0
Rev. James Lennon	10	0	0
E. Lister	10	0	0
H. R. W. A. Willis	10	0	0
Horace Walker	10	0	0
County Constabulary, by Superintendent Bent ...	10	0	0
H. Harrison	10	0	0
Crow Orchard Colliery Co.	10	0	0
Workpeople at G. Hargreaves & Co.'s, Accrington	10	0	0
Workpeople, Clifton Collieries, Workington ...	9	12	9
St. James's Church, Wigan	9	19	0
Collected by E. T. Wright	9	10	0
Peterborough Subscriptions	9	8	1
Folkestone Subscriptions	9	8	0
Employés at Pearson and Knowles's Iron Works, Moss Side	9	7	3
Burtonwood Chapel	9	6	0
St. George's Church, Chorley	9	6	0
Workpeople, Bell Bros., Limited, Middlesborough	9	5	11
Sankey Church (Morning Offertory)	9	0	0
St. Paul's, Warrington	9	0	0
J. Kitto, Llanidloes	8	18	7
St. James's Church, Congleton (per F. E. Hopwood)	8	15	0
Haigh and Aspull Parish Church	8	13	3
Brancepeth Church and Waterhouse Mission Chapel	8	13	2
Broughton Congregational Church, Manchester...	8	12	10
Workmen of Tyne Engine Works Company, (per J. H. Owen)	8	10	10
Scarborough Subscriptions	8	10	6
St. George's Church, Tyldesley	8	9	0
Tyldesley Chapel	8	8	6

	£	s.	d.
Workpeople at Stone and Sons' Collieries, Downall Green...	8	8	0
R. Lansdall	8	6	0
Ince Parish Church	8	5	10
Workpeople of Lamb and Moore, Wigan. ...	8	2	1
Workpeople, Tunstall Brothers, Brierfield ...	8	0	5
Union Iron Works, West Gorton	8	0	0
Workpeople, Garswood Hall Collieries	7	15	9
Methodist Free Church, Wigan	7	14	4
Workpeople, R. Stephenson and Co.'s Works, Newcastle-on-Tyne	7	13	10
Parish Church, Atherton...	7	13	0
Employés, Douglas Bank Collieries, Wigan ...	7	12	0
Employés, Vulcan Foundry Co.	7	12	0
Workpeople, Halliwell Mills, Bolton	7	10	8
Whitley and Co.'s Workpeople	7	10	6
St. Michael and All Angels', Wigan	7	10	4
Workpeople, Trefonen Colliery, Oswestry ...	7	10	2
Great Budworth Parish Church	7	7	0
United Methodist Free Church, Northwich ...	7	4	6
Golborne Congregational Church...	7	3	0
Sankey Sugar Co.'s Workmen (1st instalment) ...	7	1	3
St. Mary.s Church, Halton	7	1	0
Workpeople, New North Staffordshire Coal Co., Talk-o'-th'-Hill	7	0	8
Workpeople, Albert Colliery, Chesterfield ...	7	0	3
St. John's Church, Hazlewood	7	0	0
St. Peter's Church, Hindley	7	0	0
James Wilton	7	0	0
Workmen, Towneley Colliery	7	0	0
Collection at South Wingfield	6	17	6
Jasper, Kitchen, and Co. (2nd subscription) ...	6	17	0
Workpeople of Porritt and Sons, Helmshore ...	6	15	3
Longstone Church, Bakewell	6	15	3
Workmen, Rossendale Collieries, Newchurch ...	6	15	0
Altham Collieries, Accrington	6	14	9

	£	s.	d.
Skelmersdale Brass Band...	6	13	3
New Ferry Church (Offertory)	6	12	9
H. Whiley...	6	11	0
Tyldesley Pits	6	10	6
John Atherton	6	9	4
Leamington Subscriptions	6	8	6
Workpeople, F. Charlton and Sons	6	7	6
Workpeople, Greenfield and Balderstone Mill, Rochdale	6	4	7
Workpeople, Ellenborough Colliery, Maryport ...	6	4	3
St. Mary's Church, Lowton	6	2	10
Collection, St. Mary's, Llanwrst	6	2	0
Coal Corporation Hall, Oldham	6	0	0
S. Heyes and Friends	6	0	0
Workpeople, Wentworth Pit, near Barnsley ...	6	0	0
J. Owens	6	0	0
Broad-Clyst Parish Church, Exeter	5	18	9
Offertory, Douglas Church	5	16	8
Workpeople at Shirland Colliery...	5	15	7
Workpeople at Black Moss Colliery, Skelmersdale	5	14	6
United Methodist Free Church, Prescot... ...	5	12	9
Collected at Wharton Church, Winsford ...	5	11	10
Holy Trinity Church, Ashton	5	11	0
Balance of T. W. Legh's Majority Fund... ...	5	10	9
Brereton Colliery, near Rugeley	5	10	6
King Street Baptist Church, Wigan	5	10	0
St. Paul's, Over Tabley	5	10	0
Haydock Concert	5	6	2
Boschurch Parish Church, Shrewsbury	5	7	0
Christ Church, Eaton	5	6	0
Workpeople, Knott Mill Works, Manchester ...	5	6	0
Sheet at Haydock after Mr. Pickard's Address...	5	5	9
Workpeople at Loanhead Colliery, Edinburgh ...	5	5	8
Workmen of Hodgson and Stead, Salford ...	5	5	3
Ridgway and Crossley	5	5	0
John Kellett, Wigan	5	5	0

	£	s.	d.
Henry Farr and Son	5	5	0
John Wycherley	5	5	0
Richard Greenough	5	5	0
Bishop Claughton...	5	5	0
Evans and McClure	5	5	0
J. B. Wilson	5	5	0
Jos. Whittle	5	5	0
Wm. Collehole	5	5	0
Rev. E. Sherlock	5	5	0
Workpeople at Swinton Mill, Manchester ...	5	5	0
James Roscoe	5	5	0
Workpeople & others, Parker-street Mill, Preston	5	5	0
Bryan Henshaw	5	5	0
Rev. C. Sherlock	5	5	0
Roman Catholic Chapel, Leigh	5	5	0
James Maudsley	5	0	0
George Platt	5	0	0
Thomas Livesey	5	0	0
Collected at Dangoch, &c., Mines, near Pwllheli...	5	4	6
Rev. R. Smith, Lowton	5	4	6
Tyldesley Wesleyan Chapel	5	4	0
Crook Parish Church, Darlington	5	3	6
P. Walker and Sons' Employés	5	2	6
E. S. Braddyll	5	0	0
Rev. J. H. Thom	5	0	0
E. E. Carry	5	0	0
W. Thompson, King's Lynn	5	0	0
Henry Atkinson	5	0	0
John Dun	5	0	0
Sir C. de Hoghton, Bart.	5	0	0
Mrs. Beamont	5	0	0
Walter Ashton	5	0	0
E. Pierpoint	5	0	0
A Friend	5	0	0
J. Dickinson	5	0	0
Messrs. Armstrong and Berry	5	0	0

	£	s.	d.
Charles Lever	5	0	0
H. Stele	5	0	0
J. Green	5	0	0
H. B. R.	5	0	0
Mrs. Susan Deane...	5	0	0
A. M. Mitchell	5	0	0
Jas. Wrigley	5	0	0
Dowager Lady Stanley of Alderley	5	0	0
W. Kellett...	5	0	0
J. Pendlebury	5	0	0
J. H. Peck...	5	0	0
Rev. J. Leach	5	0	0
Littler, Atkins, and McVitie	5	0	0
Mrs. Nicholson	5	0	0
Thos. W. Lloyd	5	0	0
Rev. W. Jones	5	0	0
R. A. Leggett	5	0	0
Rev. W. Quekett, Warrington	5	0	0
Jos. Maxfield	5	0	0
A. Jones	5	0	0
Henry Woodcock	5	0	0
R. Garnett and Son	5	0	0
Wm. Pickard	5	0	0
H. Walmesley	5	0	0
John Peak...	5	0	0
W. H. Hewlett	5	0	0
E. Lewis Ashworth	5	0	0
W. Bryham, jun.	5	0	0
Walter Topping	5	0	0
Miss E. Mather	5	0	0
W. Grimshaw	5	0	0
Hon. Colin Lindsay	5	0	0
R. Houghton	5	0	0
Rev. H. Monk	5	0	0
R. Heath	5	0	0
C. F. Parr	5	0	0

	£	s.	d.
— Pearson	5	0	0
T. W. Earle, Huyton	5	0	0
Wm. Litton	5	0	0
Miss Litton	5	0	0
Alf. Greenall (in memory of his father, the late Thos. Greenall)	5	0	0
Ph. Speakman	5	0	0
H. A. Woodward	5	0	0
L. Pilkington	5	0	0
L. D. Grunke	5	0	0
Rev. Geo. Heaton	5	0	0
Collected by Mrs. Grace	5	0	0
F. Gardner	5	0	0
F. S. Gerard	5	0	0
C. F. Clark	5	0	0
E. and J. B., per C. B. F. B.	5	0	0
Roscoe and Lord	5	0	0
J. Lord and Brother	5	0	0
Mrs. E. Eccleston	5	0	0
B. J. E. (Crosbie)	5	0	0
Ince Forge Co.	5	0	0
A Friend	5	0	0
J. R. Buckton	5	0	0
Freemasons, Gilbert Greenall Lodge, No. 1250 ...	5	0	0
Rev. T. Edmondes, Cowbridge	5	0	0
A. H. Lloyd, Bletchingley	5	0	0
J. Clemson	5	0	0
J. and R. Tennant	5	0	0
T. W. Lloyd	5	0	0
Rev. C. Eves	5	0	0
Workmen, Grangemouth Coal Co.'s Collieries ...	5	0	0
Grangemouth Coal Co.	5	0	0
B. Fisher, Standish	5	0	0
Bardsley Colliery Accident and Funeral Society, Ashton-under-Lyne	5	0	0
M. Bailey	5	0	0

	£	s.	d
Thomas Wall	5	0	0
Richard Leigh	5	0	0
Birtle Colliery Club	5	0	0
Collected at Feather's Hotel, Liverpool	5	0	0
Workpeople at Wharf Street Mills, Ashton-under-Lyne	5	0	0
J. Speakman	5	0	0
Bill Posters' Association, Wigan...	5	0	0
T. Baldwin...	6	0	0
Norley Colliery Accident Society	5	0	0
Hartley Colliery	5	0	0
Subscriptions per Mayor of Stratford-on-Avon ...	5	0	0
A Friend, per. Rev. A. Brown	5	0	0
Workpeople Scot Lane Colliery, Blackrod ...	4	10	8
J. A. Black and Sons	3	3	0
B. Butler	1	1	0
E. Williams	1	1	0
J. W. Sabin	0	10	0
Mrs. Barrow	1	1	0
Bethesda Chapel, Broad Street, Pendleton ...	4	4	2
Philip Booth	1	1	0
Stafford Surplus Indian Famine Fund	4	11	0
St. Mary's Church, Sowerby	1	18	0
" Carita "	1	0	0
Aston Church Colliery	4	1	0
J. Topping	1	0	0
Burial Benefit Society, Pemberton	3	0	0
St. John's Presbyterian Church, Warrington ...	3	4	0
W. Anderson	3	0	0
M. Pearse...	1	1	0
R. J. Cooke	2	2	0
Miss Eden...	2	0	0
Rev. J. W. Smith...	0	10	0
Rev. C. Sedcroft	2	0	0
A. and Edith Wilson	1	1	0
M. A. Wilson	1	1	0

	£	s.	d.
Workmen at Dale House...	0	13	6
Pemberton Church Bridgewater Schools	3	0	4
Independent Methodist Chapel, Stubshaw Cross...	0	16	0
M. Whatmough ...	1	0	0
Mrs. Whatmough ...	0	5	0
Miss Whatmough...	0	5	0
J. Burgess	2	2	0
J. Davies, Wargrave School	2	2	0
Rev. H. Gibbon ...	1	10	0
H. Houghton	1	1	0
E. Ellis, Huddersfield	3	3	0
St. Michael's Church, Blackburn...	3	3	0
Mrs. Drummond ...	1	0	0
Workmen, Preston Grange Coal and Iron Co. ...	3	9	7
St. Augustine's College, Canterbury	2	2	0
Rev. Arthur Faber	1	1	0
Workpeople, Co-operative Store, Manchester ...	4	0	0
Rev. C. B. Barrow, Bath...	1	0	0
J. Walker, Edinburgh	0	5	0
Llandinorwic Church, Carnarvon	0	14	6
Rev. J. Meade	1	0	0
Ashmore Park Coal Company's Workpeople ...	1	5	5
Clewbury North Church ...	1	0	0
Rev. George Morris	1	1	0
S. Chad's Church, Romiley	0	17	8
Rev. C. Daman ...	1	1	0
Dunton Parish, Bucks ...	1	1	0
Rev. W. T. Sandys, Grantham ...	1	0	0
Plasedown, St. John's Parish Church, Bath ...	1	16	6
Rev. J. Lawson ...	2	0	0
Pupils of Miss Sewell, Leigh	1	5	11
Baptist Chapel, Atherton...	4	0	0
Mrs. Mary Rosher	2	2	0
Rev. W. Waych ...	1	0	0
Workpeople at Carr House Colliery, Rotherham	2	8	0
Workpeople at Hawkwell Colliery, Cinderford...	1	7	6

	£	s.	d.
Workpeople at Darfield Pottery Works, near Barnsley	2	3	4
Workpeople at Tunstall Colliery, Tunstall	1	10	0
Workpeople at J. Stott and Company's Collieries	2	17	8
Rev. G. Scratton	0	2	6
Anonymous	0	16	10
J. Warburton, Pemberton	0	10	6
Clegg's Box, Eccles	2	12	6
Workpeople at Cowbridge Firebrick Works	0	10	0
Workpeople at Leycott Colliery, Newcastle, Staffordshire	1	7	9
Workpeople at Garforth Colliery, Leeds	3	12	6
Rev. F. Martin	0	10	0
Surface Workmen at Clayton and Brooks, Norbury Colliery	2	18	7
Haydock Bowling Club	1	11	2
Workmen at Neston Collieries	3	1	0
Park Lane Chapel, Wigan	3	0	0
Mesnes Colliery	1	17	4
R. W. Marsh	1	1	0
Rosliston Church	1	9	0
Independent Methodist Chapel, Downall Green	1	11	8
Capt. Buckley Hall	1	1	0
Moorside Firebrick and Tile Company	1	14	0
Athenæum Cricket Club	1	5	0
A Friend	0	1	0
Friends by Allan Peel	2	10	0
Miles Williams	0	10	6
Little Brick Hill Church, Bletchley	0	18	6
Workmen at Carr's Colliery	3	16	9
C. J. Brewtnall	2	3	6
C. Ashurst	2	9	0
Pupils and Masters, Browne College, Birmingham	1	17	0
Mrs. Kent, Whitchurch, Salop	1	0	0
Primitive Methodist Society, Earlestown	3	11	6
James Dummachie	1	0	0

	£	s.	d.
D. Davies	1	0	0
Wesleyan Chapel, Skelmersdale	2	14	7
Wesleyan Chapel, Haydock	0	2	6
Job Sproston	0	10	0
Stratton Audley Church, Bicester	2	1	8
S. Hague	4	0	6
St. Hilda's Mission Church, Leeds	2	15	6
Golborne Street Chapel, Warrington	1	0	0
A Lady	0	11	4
"No Name,"	0	3	6
Half Collection at Byker Church, Newcastle-on-Tyne	2	4	7
Rev. E. F. E. Hankinson, King's Lynn... ...	1	0	0
S. Gant and Friends, Bredbury	1	2	8
J. Elliott	1	0	0
Archdeacon Jacobs	2	2	0
Teachers and Scholars, Bedworth Wesleyan School	1	0	0
David White	0	11	0
Workpeople at West Yorkshire Colliery, Hawden Clough	1	12	0
Workpeople at Denby Pottery, near Derby ...	3	11	3
Workpeople at South Staffordshire Colliery, West Bromwich	1	7	0
Workpeople at New Heyes Colliery, near Burslem	1	10	0
Mr. and Mrs. Millar	1	0	0
John Grime	1	1	0
Livesey and Sons	2	2	0
Barrow Collieries, Barnsley	1	10	0
Anderton Hall Collieries, Blackrod	3	5	4
Thorp's Gamber Hall Colliery, Barnsley... ...	0	10	0
Archdeacon Hornby	2	0	0
R. Singleton	0	10	0
Workpeople, White Lane Iron Co.'s Works ...	4	16	0
Bent Colliery, Darwen	0	16	0
Rev. S. Evans	0	5	0

	£	s.	d.
Alexandra Theatre, Earlestown	3	0	0
Collected by Rachael Thompson, Doncaster ...	1	2	0
Fine per Royal Society for Prevention of Cruelty to Animals	0	10	0
Mrs. J. J. Clarkson	3	0	0
E. B. Deal	2	0	0
" Received "	2	2	0
Workmen, Stafford Collieries, Barnsley	0	10	0
Workmen, The Coal Works, Barnsley	2	10	0
Workmen, Mountain Mines, Almwch	1	0	9
Workmen, Wicklow Copper Mines, Ireland ...	2	5	0
Workmen, Ubberley Hall Colliery, Bucknall ...	0	15	0
Workmen, Crook Colliery, Darlington	1	0	0
Workmen, Ballycastle Mines, Antrim	1	2	6
Workmen, Lycett Colliery, Newcastle-under-Lyne	1	12	9
Llanddoget Church, Llanwrst	0	7	1
Workpeople, Stockbridge Works, near Sheffield ...	0	11	0
Christ Church, Lancaster	4	12	0
St. Michael's, Cockerham, Garstang	4	0	0
Workpeople, Drunthorpe Collieries, Ashby-de-la-Zouch	1	18	3
Workpeople, Butterworth and Dickinson's Works, Burley	1	16	3
Workpeople, Lead Mines, Mold	1	7	0
Workpeople, B. & S. Massey's Ironworks, Openshaw	0	9	11
Workpeople, Booth Hill Mill Oldham	1	15	2
Workpeople, Asby Colliery, Arlecdon	1	12	6
Workpeople, A. Simpson, Manchester	3	3	0
Workpeople, Charity Collieries, near Nuneaton ...	4	13	0
Workpeople, Mid Cannock Colliery, Cannock ...	2	15	4
Workpeople, Hilton Colliery, Wolverhampton ...	2	3	3
Workpeople, J. Cranshaw's Colliery, Dewsbury ...	3	2	0
Eccleshill Coal Company	2	0	3
Employés, Tunnicliffe and Hampson	4	17	6
Collected by Miss Lee, Ellesmere	3	10	0

	£	s.	d.
A Friend	1	10	0
Rev. C. A. Wilkinson	1	0	0
Martha E. Glendinning	3	3	0
Workpeople, Duckworth Hall Mill	1	0	2
Workpeople, Victoria Mill, Hollinwood	2	10	4
Workpeople, Essington Farm Colliery, Bloxwich.	1	2	0
Workpeople, Throckley Colliery, Newcastle-on-Tyne	2	10	0
Workpeople, Pelsall Coal Company	2	10	0
Workpeople, Globe Ironworks, Liverpool ...	1	6	3
Workpeople, Whitehaven Fire Brick, &c., Works	2	0	0
Workpeople, Wigpool Mines, Mitcheldean ...	0	8	0
J. Maddock	2	2	0
W. Smith and Co	1	11	8
Workpeople of W. Smith and Co.	3	8	4
Workpeople of William Gill Colliery, Arking-withdale	1	3	0
Workpeople of Urpeth Colliery, Durham ...	3	10	0
Workpeople of Dean Mills, Rumworth	1	8	6
Workpeople of Llangewich Collieries, Llanelly ...	1	1	6
Workpeople of Pendleton Alum Works... ...	1	13	0
Workpeople of New Hucknall Colliery, Mansfield	1	8	6
Wesleyan Methodist Chapel, Weaverham ...	1	3	0
Rev. A. D. Spong...	0	10	0
Bennett Brothers, Liverpool	2	10	0
C. B. Robinson	1	1	0
J. S. Walker and Brothers	3	3	0
Workpeople of Drainage Company, Holywell ...	1	10	0
Brookside Mill, Oswaldtwistle	2	10	0
Bettisfield Colliery, Bagillt	1	1	3
Newbury Collieries, Somerset	1	14	6
Holdsworth Brothers	2	5	9
Coleshill Colliery, Flint	0	19	6
Medlock Mills, Oldham	2	5	0
Yew Tree Ironworks, Hollinwood	1	0	11
Workpeople, J. Lord and Sons	1	6	6

	£	s.	d.
Workpeople, Blackpool Colliery	1	19	0
Workpeople, Blackfield Colliery	1	14	6
Collection at Leigh Methodist Chapel	3	5	7
Collection at Glazebrook Methodist Chapel ...	2	2	9
Collection at Glazebury Methodist Chapel ...	0	18 ·	0
Collection at Edgegreen Methodist Chapel ...	2	6	10
Collection at Platt Bridge Methodist Chapel ...	1	2	0
Collection at Stubshaw Cross Methodist Chapel...	2	8	4
J. Glover	0	2	6
United Methodist Free Church, Shwelach ...	0	15	4
Newton Town Hall Boxes	3	3	8
Mayor of Buckingham	1	10	0
Workpeople, Longworth Mill	0	15	0
Worpeople, Wier and Irwell Mills, Bacup ...	1	1	8
Workpeople, Moss-side Mills, Pendlebury ...	1	10	0
Workpeople, Boythorpe Colliery, Chesterfield ...	4	11	6
Workpeople, North Foundry, Liverpool... ...	1	16	9
Workpeople, Gaghills Mills, Waterfoot	2	8	3
Workpeople, Planing and Moulding Mills, Raw-			
tenstall	1	4	0
Workpeople, Butler Green Spinning Co., Limited	2	5	6
Workpeople, Phœnix Mills, Bolton	1	7	10
Workpeople, Knott Mill Ironworks, Manchester	1	15	6
Workpeople, Smithfield Mill, Burnley	0	11	8
Workpeople, The Tileries, Tunstall	4	0	0
Workpeople, Rakswood Co-operative Society,			
Limited	1	0	0
Cirencester Congregational Chapel	0	10	0
Workpeople, East Black Craig Mine, Newton			
Stewart	0	18	0
Workpeople, Bridgewater Foundry, Swinton ...	1	10	5
Workpeople, Canada Works, Birkenhead ...	1	1	0
Workpeople, Robert Gilchrist and Co.	0	16	0
Workpeople, Oldham Boilerworks Company ...	1	14	3
Workpeople, Moscow Mills, Church	3	13	0
Workpeople, F. Rigby and Co., Westhoughton...	0	14	0

	£	s.	d.
Workpeople, Sovereign Mills, Wigan	2	16	6
Workpeople, Wellington Mills, Great Lever ...	3	7	8
A Friend of H. Rowlands	0	8	8
A Friend	0	2	6
J. Milne	0	5	0
Workpeople, Broomhill Colliery, Adlington ...	3	8	0
Mrs. Sheldon, Bishop's Fonthill Rectory, Salisbury	1	1	0
Johnson, Johnson and Gordon	0	3	0
Andrew and Aspinall Hurst	0	3	6
Otto Freehman	3	3	0
Shirland Church	3	0	0
J. Sedward...	1	1	0
Bright and Legge	1	1	0
Mrs. Thompson	1	0	0
T. Smith	1	1	0
Mrs. Corbett's Box	3	7	6
Workpeople, Haigh Foundry	0	10	4
Workpeople, New Road Spinning Co., Limited...	0	15	0
Workpeople, Gamant Collieries, near Llanelly ...	3	2	0
Llanwrst Tabernacle	1	14	0
Eyton Co-operative Company	0	11	4
Concert at Chorley	0	10	4
Jarrow Colliery, Castle Corner Co., Kilkenny ...	4	10	0
Workpeople, Harsham Colliery, near Bristol ...	0	12	4
Workpeople, Woodside Colliery, Carluke ...	2	2	0
Workpeople, Naylor-street Ironworks, Liverpool	3	5	0
United Methodist Free Church School, Leigh, Lancashire	2	18	6
Crosshillock Pits	2	13	9
Workpeople, Park Place Mill, Blackburn ...	0	6	3
Workpeople, Alexander Mill, Bury	2	0	0
Workpeople, Brownlow Fold Mills, Bolton ...	2	18	0
Workpeople, Dunkirk Collieries, Dukinfield ...	2	19	11
Workpeople, Quinta Collieries, Chirk	1	7	0
A Friend at Hindley, per W. Harris	0	4	0

	£	s.	d.
A Friend	0	2	6
Workpeople, Clanwilliam Slate Quarry, Wooden Bridge Company, Wicklow	1	0	0
Workpeople, Sandwell Park Colliery	0	12	5
Workpeople, Gwam Cae Gwewae Colliery, Llanelly	1	19	9
Workpeople, North Ironworks, Waterfoot ...	1	5	6
J. Macbeth	0	10	0
G. Cusons	0	5	0
T. and T. Vicars	1	14	9
Workpeople, Lofthouse Station Colliery... ...	2	15	8
Workpeople, Rushton Mines, Isle of Man ...	1	8	1
Workpeople, Ibstock Colliery	2	5	0
Workpeople, Nelson Mills, Bolton	3	3	0
Molyneux's Box	0	5	0
Workpeople, Tong Mill	1	16	2
Workpeople, Britannia Foundry, Bolton ...	1	10	3
Workpeople, Alma Mills, Oldham	0	17	4
Workpeople, Goole Pellas Mine, St. Ives ...	1	10	0
Workpeople, Gladstone Spinning Co., Failsworth	1	14	0
Workpeople, Farrett's Collieries, Bath	3	16	6
Workpeople, Longworth and Sons, Whalley ...	2	10	0
Mayor of Hertford	1	1	0
Rev. J. Cole, Exeter	0	10	0
— Barr, Earlestown	0	5	0
Mrs. Burdis, Newton	0	5	0
Rev. O. Churchyard	0	2	6
Nant y Ghrew Chapel, Llanwrst...	0	13	6
Mayor of Hastings	2	2	0
A Friend, Hastings	0	10	0
Workpeople at South Skelton, Johnstone Mines, Gainsborough	4	15	0
United Methodist Free Churches, Liverpool, (North Circuit)	4	6	7
West Hatton Church, Brigg, Lincolnshire ...	0	10	6
H. B.	1	0	0
Workpeople, Ellerbeck Colliery, Coppull ...	4	17	0

	£	s.	d.
Employés of J. W. Stead, Salford	1	6	6
Collection at Hope Congregational Chapel, Nelson	1	10	0
Workpeople at Florence Colliery, Longton, Staffordshire	1	15	0
Christ Church, Pendlebury	0	10	0
Rev. T. Turnbull	0	3	0
Workpeople, Weir Bridge Mill, Wigan	0	15	0
Workpeople, Vicaro, Steel-street, Liverpool ...	2	12	5
Workpeople, Victoria Mill, Lowton	2	8	6
Workpeople, Burnley Ironworks...	2	15	9
Workpeople, Walsall Wood Colliery	2	2	6
Workpeople, Victoria Mill, Patricroft	2	12	3
Workpeople, Spring Mill, Mossley	1	2	3
Workpeople, Bridge and Quarry-street Mills, Stalybridge	2	7	2
Workpeople, Laister Dyke Colliery, near Bradford	0	10	0
Workpeople, Castleton Tower Mills, Rochdale ...	1	10	0
Workpeople, Clarington Brook Forge, Ince ...	1	18	6
Workpeople, Cookstown Mines	2	10	0
Workpeople, New Rhos Colliery, Pongarn ...	1	2	6
Workpeople, Mill Hill Spinning Co., Bolton-le-Moors...	0	13	9
Workpeople, Britannia Foundry, Bury-street, Salford	1	18	4
Workpeople, Phœnix Mill, Little Lever ...	1	16	2
Warkpeople, Upper Mill, Golborne	1	15	0
Workpeople, Brotherton Mill, Rochdale ...	1	6	10
Workpeople, Well Bank Mill, Bolton	0	13	6
Workpeople, Lime Mill, Hollinwood	2	2	7
Workpeople, Horsley Colliery, Wylam-on-Tyne	1	7	0
Workpeople, Schofield Street, and Albert Mills, Heywood	2	6	0
Workpeople, Cambrian Slate Co.'s Quarries, Chester	4	3	9

	£	s.	d.
Workpeople, Small Iron Foundry, Clodwich, Oldham	0	5	0
Collected at Godney Church, Somerset	3	8	0
Collected at Independent Methodist Chapel, Lamberhead Green	2	0	0
Collected at Methodist Free Church, Pemberton	0	14	1
Collected at St. Helens, Bishop Auckland ...	1	11	6
Per O. E. Raymond, Balmer, Sudbury	0	5	0
H. G. Haig, Andover	1	0	0
Workpeople, Robinson, Son, and Rimmer ...	1	1	0
Hollins Brothers and Co....	2	2	0
St. Andrew's Church, Beamish	2	10	8
St. James's Church, Burnsfield	2	10	8
T. and C. H. Arrowsmith, Astley	0	10	0
Snydal Church, Ulverston	2	6	9
Micklethwaite's Sewing Class, Ulverston ...	0	7	0
Rev. W. T. Radford, Basingstoke	1	0	0
Canon Turner, Chester	1	1	0
Rev. C. J. Chittenden, Capel Curig	0	5	0
Rev. T. Nevin, Normanton	0	5	0
Hundall Colliery	0	12	0
Dunn and Sons, Ancoats	2	8	4
Newtown Mill, Bromley	1	10	0
Workmen, West Hartley Colliery, Nidderton ...	0	15	3
Workmen, Union Mill, Openshaw	1	8	0
Workmen, Smallbridge Mill, Rochdale	1	11	5
Workmen, Peel Park Manufacturing Company, Pendleton	2	7	6
Workmen, Union Bridge Ironworks, Manchester	2	7	7
Workmen, Cannock and Seacroft Colliery ...	2	1	0
Workmen, Henrietta Street Ironworks, Bacup...	0	17	1
Workmen, Union Mill, Royton	2	0	0
Workmen, Portland Street Mills, Ashton-under-Lyne	1	0	0
Workmen, Robert Street Foundry, Darwen ...	1	0	0

	£	s.	d.
Workmen, Greenhalgh and Harrison's Mill, Ramsbottom	1	10	0
Workmen, Leeds Patent Brickworks	0	10	6
Workmen, Vale Mills, Shaw	0	15	7
Workmen, A. and J. Hoyle's Mill, Radcliffe ...	3	0	0
J. J. Wigan	1	0	0
Gateshead Mutual Improvement Society ...	3	12	4
Box, Derby Arms, Prescot	0	7	6
Employès Alliance Coal Company	1	17	0
Belle Green Mission Church	1	7	6
Hall of Ince Church	0	12	11
E. Hipwood and Friends, Kibworth	0	14	0
Workpeople, Wharncliffe and Silkstone Collieries, Wortley	0	17	5
Workpeople, Pemberton Colliery	2	18	5
Workpeople, Shaw Spinning Co., Oldham ...	1	5	0
Workpeople, Coney Colliery, Over Darwen ...	0	10	0
Workpeople, Moat Hall Colliery, Shrewsbury ...	3	0	0
Workpeople, Primrose Mill, Church	1	6	0
Workpeople, Rochdale Co-operative Society, Mitchell Hey Mills	1	0	0
Offertory at Luddendenfoot	0	13	6
Rev. H. Farnlanx, Heyford	0	10	0
Haydock Good Templars	2	16	4
Miss Fairclongh	3	0	0
A Widow	0	3	6
Orrell Congregational Chapel, Wigan	2	10	0
Richard Hunt	1	0	0
Collected by Mrs. Barclay, Earlestown	0	9	1
Flint Glass Makers, Warrington...	1	15	6
J. Slaney	1	0	0
Mrs. Slaney ... —	0	10	0
J. H. Slaney	0	10	0
St. Peter's Offertory	1	7	0
A. B. C., Falmouth	1	0	0
W. Critchley	0	10	0

	£	s.	d.
P.O.O.	1	0	0
W. Sharp	3	3	0
John Abraham	1	1	0
J. C.	0	10	0
T. Winstanley	0	10	0
St. Bartholomew's Church, Rainhill	2	0	0
John Davies	3	3	0
R. Guest and Mrs. Guest	2	2	0
S. Plitts	0	10	0
J. Lawrence and Sons	2	2	0
John Laycock	1	1	0
J. L. Smith	2	2	0
J. T. Freeman	1	1	0
Cecil de Trafford	3	0	0
Ebenezer Chapel, Warrington	1	1	6
Canon Brandreth	2	2	0
Thomas Milligan	2	2	0
Anonymous, Bowden	3	3	0
M. A. Giblin	1	0	0
J. W.	1	0	0
B. C.	0	10	0
"Box"	0	12	9
E. Davies's Workmen	1	1	0
A. Evans	2	0	0
Sums per George Wiley	3	12	6
Mrs. Barton, Cross Lane	3	0	0
A. Edwards	0	10	0
A Derby Collier, per "Sheffield Telegraph" ...	0	2	0
John Williamson	0	5	0
H. Jackson	0	10	0
Abram Chutch	4	13	0
Hartford Wesleyan Chapel	4	0	0
Warburton Church	4	14	7
Edward Ashton	0	10	0
J. A. H.	0	3	0
S. B.	0	2	6

	£	s.	d.
F. R.	0	2	6
W. Grimshaw	1	0	0
A Friend, Helensburgh	1	0	0
Box, Royal Hotel, Southport	4	0	6
C. A. Williams	1	0	0
Walter Butler, Llandudno	2	2	0
Baptist Chapel, Leigh	2	0	0
Thomas Mather, Croft	1	0	0
Rev. G. Feather	3	5	0
Boxes at Newton Bridge and Town Hall ...	2	18	8
Rev. G. W. Griffith	1	1	0
Geo. A. Smith	1	0	0
Rev. T. P. Kirkman	3	0	0
Mrs. Butler, per C. Pilkington	4	0	0
Miss Butler	1	0	0
Thomas Middlemore	1	1	0
F. F. Tucker	1	0	0
Mrs. Corbetts, (1d. Subscriptions)	3	0	0
E. Booth	1	1	0
St. Mary's, Latchford	3	12	5
Holy Trinity Church, Warrington	4	1	3
Pemberton Iron Church	3	17	2
St. Paul's Church, Pemberton	1	9	6
Far Moor Church, Orrell	1	3	3
Mrs. Hedley	4	3	0
J. L. Hedley	3	3	0
Mayor of Ryde	1	1	0
Anonymous Sums...	0	11	8
Salt Lane Mill, Brierfield	1	3	9
Workpeople, Barrack Street Mills, Burnley ...	0	7	3
Workpeople, Neville Hill Collieries, Leeds ...	3	5	6
Workpeople, Sovereign Mills, Preston	1	7	3
Workpeople, J. and C. H. Arrowsmith's ...	2	8	8
Workpeople, India Mills Spinning Co., Darwen	2	19	8
Workpeople, J. and W. Bourne's, Brindle Mill, Chorley	2	0	0

	£	s.	d.
Workpeople, Albert Mill, Unsworth	1	10	0
Workpeople, Beard, Bupworth, and Shallcross ...	4	2	3
Workpeople, Seed Hill Mill, Nelson	1	6	0
Workpeople, New Sister, &c., Collieries, Little Hulton	4	3	0
Workpeople, Hathershaw Mill, Oldham ...	1	15	2
Workpeople, Manufacturing Company, Limited, Haslingden	2	10	0
Workpeople, Bardsley Mill, Ashton	1	10	0
Egyptian Lodge, No. 27	2	0	0
Fine from a Collier for wilfully damaging a lamp whilst at work, at Clayton and Brooks' Collieries, Stockport	2	0	0
Grassmore Collieries	1	1	6
Men at Adelaide Colliery, Durham	1	2	6
Employés of J. S. Garland	0	11	0
Liverpool Commercial Bank	4	19	1
Piddletreuthide Church	3	10	0
Workpeople, Hatherton Colliery, Bloxwich ...	0	15	6
Moiety of Penalties from County Magistrates ...	0	15	0
Collected at Grosvenor Hotel, Chester	1	1	3
Collection at Gateshead Baptist Chapel	2	5	0
Workpeople, Brock Mill Forge	0	3	9
R. Barker	0	5	0
St. Thomas's Church, Bedford	2	0	0
Workpeople, South Garesfield Colliery, Durham	1	0	4
St. Paul's Schools, Hindley	1	6	0
G. Draper	1	0	0
Workpeople Endemundsley Collieries	1	0	0
Captain Brown	1	0	0
Miss Ormrod's School Children	0	2	2
J. H. Parkinson and Son	3	3	0
Employés at Runcorn Railway Station	1	3	6
Pont Bluddgn Church	0	17	0
St. Luke's Mission, Stubshaw Cross	2	2	2
Gospel Tent, Prescot	4	2	0

	£	s.	d.
John Naylor	1	1	0
Major Legge	1	0	0
Superintendent Clarkson	1	0	0
Miss McCorquodale	1	0	0
Miss Kate McCorquodale	0	10	0
John Devereux	0	10	0
D. F. Ramsey	1	0	0
Golborne Wesleyan Society	3	0	7
T. Boustead	1	1	0
J. Platt	2	0	0
William Lowe	1	1	0
Welsh Church, Wigan	1	13	0
James Logan, Manchester	1	1	0
Burley (Yorkshire) Parish Church	4	11	6
Zion Chapel, Prescot	3	0	0
Thomas Hunt	3	0	0
A. P. Rose...	0	11	5
Mrs. Wardell	2	2	0
A Friend per J. H. Owen	0	15	0
Rev. J. D. Middleton	1	1	0
Great Broughton Congregational Church, Chester	1	12	10
St. Stephen's Church, Congleton...	2	13	10
F. Scott	1	3	0
David Smith	1	0	0
John Grunke	2	0	0
S. F. Kelley	4	0	0
A Friend	0	5	0
G. Kirkwound	2	2	0
Henri Schielard	1	19	3
G. W. Wrigley	1	0	0
Pemberton Colliery Iron Church (in addition) ...	0	10	0
Alms Box, Christ Church, Ashton-under-Lyne, per J. D. Kelley	2	0	10
Hindley Particular Baptist Chapel	3	0	6
Thompson and Swaine	2	2	0
Box, King's Arms Inn, Prescot, per E. L. Lloyd.	1	1	0

	£	s.	d.
William Chadwick	2	2	0
George Godwin	3	3	0
Working Men's Mission, Bank Quay	2	17	4
J. Robinson	1	0	0
James Winstanley	1	1	0
J. F.	1	0	0
A Friend	1	0	0
Mrs. Jane Legh	1	0	0
Richard Greenough, jun.	0	10	0
Workpeople at R. Greenough, jun.'s, Leigh ...	0	11	6
St. James's Church, Manchester	0	7	8
Winwick Parish Church	2	8	6
St. Margaret's, Pennington Green	3	4	0
St. John the Baptist's, New Springs	2	17	11
Pendleton Ragged School...	1	2	8
St. Thomas's Church, Wigan	2	14	2
Unitarian Church, Astley...	2	2	0
A Friend, High Legh	0	5	0
Wrenbury Church...	4	13	0
St. James's Sunday Schools, Latchford	2	7	6
St. James's Mission Church, Atherton	3	17	6
Wood Rock Parish Church, Wakefield	3	9	2
Newton Commissioners' Workmen, per R. Brierley	3	5	0
Rev. M. Stapylton	1	2	0
A. B. Haslam	0	10	0
Boxes at Newton Bridge and Town Hall ...	2	3	1
Welsh Chapel, Earlestown	3	5	6
Welsh Chapel, Sutton	0	10	0
T. Laithwaite	2	0	0
Scholars' Subscriptions, per James Taylor ...	1	16	6
Jesper, Kitching, and Co.	3	3	0
"Nil Desperandum," Runcorn	1	0	0
"Light and Dark Company," Theatre Royal, Runcorn	3	1	9
E. Milner	2	2	0

	£	s.	d.
SS. Michael and All Angels' Church, Wigan (Children's Service)	0	11	10
Padgate Church	4	9	6
Mission Tent, Earlestown...	1	15	0
Rev. Prebendary Stephenson	0	5	0
Prescot Cricket Club	2	12	3
W. R. Metcalfe	1	0	0
Joe Coop	1	0	0
Holy Trinity, Bollington	4	17	8
— Parry's Underground Men	1	2	9
Norley Coal and Cannel Co.'s Workpeople ...	2	9	8
G. Chalmers, by Mr. McCorquodale	4	0	0
Visitors, Colwyn Bay	1	5	6
Rev. J. Allatt	1	1	0
J. Bates's Workpeople, Bilston	0	10	0
Dr. Owen, Llangefin	1	0	0
Charlestown Brick and Tile Co.'s Workpeople ...	0	11	0
Rev. Henry-Stobart, Workington	2	0	0
A. M. P. (Rev. William Preston)	1	0	0
Rev. H. S. Eyre	1	0	0
Dr. C. A. Heartley	3	0	0
Leigh Cricket Club	3	7	2
St. Peter's Mission Church, Leigh	2	13	0
Independent Methodist Chapel, Lowton Common	2	4	2
A. Friend, Warrington	1	0	0
C. B. and Co.	2	0	0
A. T. and Co.	1	1	0
H. and F.	1	1	0
C. L. M.	0	10	6
P. and J.	0	5	0
S. B. and Co.	1	1	0
J. R. P. and Co.	0	10	6
P. P. and Co.	0	5	0
G. Leviston	1	0	0
Collecting Box	0	3	6
Miss Ross	0	2	6

	£	s.	d.
Rev. H. A. Hignett	4	5	0
G. A. Langdale	1	1	0
Church Collection, Duke's Club, per Canon Barclay	3	10	1
W. R. C. Rogers	1	0	0
All Saints' Girls' School, Hindley	0	3	9
Tyldesley Congregational Church	3	18	0
Mrs. Clough	0	10	0
Miss Danbey	0	10	0
Wargrave School	0	11	6
R. W.	0	10	0
J. Bickerstaffe	1	1	0

HAYDOCK COLLIERY EXPLOSION RELIEF FUND.

STATEMENT OF RECEIPTS AND PAYMENTS TO 31st MARCH, 1879.

RECEIPTS.	£	s.	d.	£	s.	d.
Subscriptions—						
Paid to Parr's Banking Co., Limited, Warrington	23200	4	9			
Paid to Parr's Banking Co., Limited, St. Helens	2119	14	7			
				25319	19	4
Bank Interest, less Commission				265	8	11
				£25585	8	3

PAYMENTS.	£	s.	d.	£	s.	d.
Relief of Widows	601	8	6			
„ Children	1110	16	0			
				1712	4	6
Printing, Advertising, Postage, &c....	527	18	2			
Pay Clerk and Assistants...	184	15	0			
Travelling and Incidental Expenses...	85	4	8			
Salary of Secretary	25	0	0			
Gift to Secretary	100	0	0			
				922	17	10
Balance in hand, namely,						
Parr's Banking Co., Limited, Warrington	20820	11	4			
Parr's Banking Co., Limited, St. Helens...	2119	14	7			
Secretary	10	0	0			
				22950	5	11
				£25585	8	3

Audited, 19th May, 1879.
HOLMES & JOHNSON, Accountants,
Wigan.

The Relief Fund, Postscript.

For some time it was a mystery what happened to the Haydock Relief Fund. Perhaps there was a large amount of money resting in a bank accruing interest which could be given to no one as all the possible recipients were now dead. The answer was found while the authors were ploughing their way though local papers looking for references to the local pits. In the *'Newton and Earlestown Guardian'* dated 28th. February, 1930. The headlines were to announce the next mining disaster in Haydock and, fortunately the next after the Wood Pit disaster. This was at Lyme Pit where thirteen men were to loose their lives. There were banner headlines *'Lyme Pits Disaster'*. Inside the same paper there was a small part of a column which caught their eye. It said *'Haydock Explosion Fund'* and went on to announced that the residue of the Haydock Explosion Fund which had been set up to help the widows and orphans of the Wood Pit Disaster of 1878 had been donated to The Lancashire and Cheshire Miners' Association.

Postscript.

Many people of Haydock wished to see a permanent memorial to the village's heritage and to the victims of the Wood Pit Explosion. Among these were Councillor Jim Caunce has served the people of Haydock for many years in Local Government. Over those long years he had also tended the St. James' graveyard with love and care and the idea a lasting memorial to the men of the Wood Pit was very dear to him. With the help of the Lancashire National Union of Mineworkers and British Coal his wish came true. Jim attended in his official capacity as Mayor of St. Helens, an office he was holding for the second time.

The church was packed on that Whit Sunday, 7th. June, 1992 and the atmosphere was charged with memories and emotion and the Reverend David Shepphard, Lord Bishop of Liverpool, recalled the mining heritage of the village in a very moving address.

This was many of the extraordinary coincidences that life throws up. Another was the dedication of the Wood Pit Memorial at St. James, Haydock on 7th. June 1992 by the Revered David Shepphard, The Lord Bishop of Liverpool. This was one hundred and fourteen years to the day of the disaster and by another coincidence was a Whit Sunday as was the Sunday following the explosion in 1878.

NATIONAL UNION OF MINEWORKERS
LANCASHIRE AREA

MEMORIAL SERVICE

and

DEDICATION

of a

MEMORIAL

To commemorate

The Wood Pit Mining Disaster

7th June, 1878

and

ALL OTHER MINEWORKERS WHO DIED IN THE
COLLIERIES OF HAYDOCK

———::———

DEDICATION BY:

The Lord Bishop of Liverpool. The Rt. Revd. DAVID SHEPPARD on Sunday 7th June, 1992 at 1.00 p.m. at St. James the Great Church, Haydock.

In the presence of the Mayor of St. Helens: Cllr. JAMES CAUNCE

THE MEMORIAL

The Memorial erected in the Churchyard of St. James the Great, Haydock, takes the form of a "wayside" Crusifix. The inscription, printed below, is self explanatory.

We have been fortunate to be able to welcome the Bishop of Liverpool on Whitsunday for the dedication of the Memorial, since the 7th June is the Anniversary of the Wood Pit explosion.

The beginning of the inscription is inspired by a poem written after the disaster in 1878.

Thanks are owing to:-

Varty's Monumental Masons, Ince, who have constructed the monument.

Wiswell's of Haydock who have made the Cross out of oak.

The Haydock Brass Band playing at the Service.

The Parkside Colliery Choir also assisting at the Service.

Inside the Church building there is an illuminated list of those who are actually buried on the site of the Cross. Others killed in the Wood Pit explosion are interred elsewhere in the district. The illuminated manuscript has been beautifully produced by Mr. Ernest Holden, a retired miner; and by the kind offices of Mr. Ian Winstanley, the author of a book on the Wood Pit disaster.

———::———

"WEEP MOTHERS WEEP"

ERECTED TO THE MEMORY OF THE MEN, WOMEN AND BOYS WHO LOST THEIR LIVES IN THE HAYDOCK COLLIERIES; AND TO THOSE VICTIMS OF THE WOOD PIT EXPLOSION ON 7TH JUNE, 1878, WHO LIE AT REST ON THIS SITE.

Placed by the Lancashire Area N.U.M. and British Coal Corporation North West Group.

Dedicated 7th June, 1992 by the Rt. Revd. David Sheppard, Bishop of Liverpool.

ORDER OF SERVICE

—::—

Welcome by the Vicar of St. James The Great Church, Haydock, The Revd. Paul Nener.

As the Bishop and other Clergy enter we all sing the Whitsuntide Hymn:
  Come down, O Love divine.

> Come down, O Love divine,
> seek thou this soul of mine,
> and visit it with thine own ardour glowing;
> O Comforter, draw near,
> within my heart appear,
> and kindle it, thy holy flame bestowing.
>
> O let it freely burn,
> till earthly passions turn
> to dust and ashes in its heat consuming;
> and let thy glorious light
> shine 'ever on my sight,
> and clothe me round the while my path illuming.
>
> Let holy Charity
> mine outward vesture be,
> and lowliness become mine inner clothing:
> true lowliness of heart,
> which takes the humbler part,
> and o'er its own shortcomings weep with loathing.
>
> And so the yearning strong,
> with which the soul will long,
> shall far outpass the power of human telling;
> for none can guess the grace,
> till he become the place
> wherein the Holy Spirit makes his dwelling.

Priest: In the Name of the Father, and of the Son, and of the Holy Spirit

ALL: AMEN

The Lord be with you

ALL: AND ALSO WITH YOU

OPENING PRAYER

ALL SIT   A Reading from the Book of Job
Chapter 38, verses 4 - 7

Read by Mr. Roy Jackson, General Secretary of the Lancashire Mineworkers' Union.

Then the Lord answered Job:
"Where were you when I laid the foundation of the earth?
Tell me if you have understanding.
Who determined its measurements - surely you know!
Or who stretched the line upon it?
On what were its bases sunk, or who laid its cornerstones when the morning stars sang together, and all the sons of God shouted for joy?"

Reader: This is the word of the Lord

ALL: THANKS BE TO GOD
A Reading from the Letter of St. Paul to the Ephesians, Chapter 6, verses 13 - 17.

Read by Mrs. Marie Rimmer, Leader of St. Helens Metropolitan Borough Council.

Take the whole armour of God, that you may be able to stand in the evil day.
Stand therefore having girded your loins with truth;
and having put on the breastplate of righteousness, and having shod your feet with the equipment of the Gospel of peace;
beside all these taking the shield of faith, with which you can quench all the fiery darts of the evil one.
And taking the sword of the Spirit, which is the word of God.

Reader: This is the word of the Lord

ALL: THANKS BE TO GOD

HYMN

Guide me, O thou great Redeemer,
pilgrim through this promised land;
I am weak, but thou art mighty;
hold me with thy powerful hand:
    bread of heaven,
feed me now and evermore.

Open now the crystal fountain
whence the healing stream doth flow;
let the fiery, cloudy pillar
lead me all my journey through:
    strong deliverer,
be thou still my strength and shield.

When I tread the verge of Jordan,
bid my anxious fears subside;
death of death, and hell's destruction,
land me safe on Canaan's side:
    songs and praises,
I will ever give to thee.

REMAIN STANDING FOR THE READING FROM THE GOSPEL

Reader: The Revd. Tom Kennedy, Parish Priest,
English Martyrs Church, Haydock.

A Reading from the Holy Gospel according to St. John,
Chapter 13, verses 34 - 38.

ALL: GLORY TO CHRIST OUR SAVIOUR
Jesus said,

"A new commandment I give to you, that you love one another, even as I have loved you, that you love one another. By this shall all men know that you are my disciples, if you have love one for another."
Simon Peter said to him,
"Lord, where are you going?"
Jesus answered,
"Where I am going you cannot follow now, but you shall follow afterwards".
Peter said to him,
"Lord, why cannot I follow you now? I will lay down my life for you."
Jesus answered,
"Will you lay down your life for me?
truly I say to you, the cock will not crow till you have denied me three times."

Reader: This is the Gospel of Christ

ALL: PRAISE TO CHRIST OUR LORD

THE ADDRESS

The Rt. Revd. David Sheppard, The Bishop of Liverpool

After the Address the Parkside Colliery Choir will lead the Hymn
"The Old Rugged Cross"

(During this Hymn there will be a Collection for expenses)

On a hill far away,
stood an old rugged Cross,
the emblem of suffering and shame:
and I loved that old Cross,
where the dearest and best
for a world of lost sinners was slain:

So I'll cherish the old rugged Cross
'till my trophies at last I lay down:
I will cling to the old rugged Cross
and exchange it some day for a crown.

Oh that old rugged Cross,
so despised by the world,
has a wondrous attraction for me:
for the dear Lamb of God
left his glory above,
to bear it to dark Calvary:

In the old rugged Cross,
stained with blood so divine,
a wondrous beauty I see:
for 'twas on that old Cross
Jesus suffered and died
to pardon and sanctify me:

To the old rugged Cross
I will ever be true,
its shame and reproach gladly bear
Then he'll call me some day
to my home far away,
there his glory for ever I'll share:

THE PRAYERS

Conducted by the Revd. Norman Pine, Haydock Methodist Chapel.

ALL KNEEL: PRAYERS CONCLUDE WITH THE
LORD'S PRAYER.

At the end of the Prayers we all sit while the Parkside Colliery Choir sings.

DEUS SALUTIS ... ... arr. Mansel Thomas

After the Hymn ALL KNEEL for the Bishop's Blessing.

We then all move to the Churchyard for the Dedication of the Memorial.

——::——

On arrival at the Memorial the Bishops says:-
The Lord be with you

ALL: AND ALSO WITH YOU

Bishop: Father Almighty and everlasting God, you have shown
your eternal love to us by the Passion, death and Resurrec-
tion of your dear Son, Jesus Christ.
We pray that all who look on his Cross mayfind something
of your great love for the world, and be led to the worship
of you, our loving God.
We make our prayer through Jesus Christ our Lord.

ALL: AMEN.

The Bishop blesses the Cross.
Almighty God our heavenly Father,
Bless, sanctify and hallow this memorial and make it holy.
May it stand here for ever as a sign of the great love that
it shows, and may all those whom it commemorates rest in
peace and rise into the glory and peace of your eternal
kingdom.

We ask this for the sake of Jesus Christ the Lord.

ALL: AMEN.

HYMN   When I survey the wondrous Cross, on which the Prince
of glory died, my richest gain I count but loss and pour
contempt on all my pride.

Forbid it, Lord, that I should boast
save in the Cross of Christ my God;
all the vain things that charm me most,
I sacrifice them to his blood.

See from his head, his hands, his feet,
sorrow and love flow mingling down;
did e'er such love and sorrow meet,
or thorns compose so rich a crown?

Were the whole realm of nature mine,
that were an offering far too small;
love so amazing, so divine,
demands my soul, my life, my all.

Bishop: The Lord be with you

ALL: AND ALSO WITH YOU

Go in peace to love and serve the Lord

ALL: IN THE NAME OF CHRIST, AMEN.

ALL: THE GRACE OF OUR LORD JESUS CHRIST, AND
THE LOVE OF GOD, AND THE FELLOWSHIP OF
THE HOLY SPIRIT, BE WITH US ALL NOW AND
EVERMORE.   AMEN.

"WEEP MOTHERS WEEP"

Lines suggested by the Colliery explosion at Haydock June 7th 1878 in which 200 precious lives were lost.

This anonymous ballad was composed after the explosion and sold as a penny broadsheet to raise money for the widows and orphans.

VERSES I AND II:

Weep Mothers, weep o'er the loss of your dear ones
The Fathers and Children who are strewn amongst the dead,
The Explosion has fill'd the whole district with sadness
For homes that are lonely, and hearts that have bled.

There are sorrowing ones in the neighbourhood of Haydock,
God grant to them, his help may be given;
Though the present be dark may Hope fill the bosom,
That at last they shall meet with their lov'd ones in Heaven.

The Ceremony of Dedication.

Father Paul Nener,
John Evans, M.P.,
Elsie Caunce,
Rt. Rev. David Shepphard,
Cllr. Jim Caunce,
John Newton, Free Church Moderator.
Father Kennedy.

The Wood Pit Memorial, Haydock.

"WEEP MOTHERS, WEEP"
ERECTED TO THE MEMORY OF
THE MEN, WOMEN AND BOYS WHO LOST
THEIR LIVES IN THE HAYDOCK COLLIERIES;
AND TO THOSE VICTIMS OF THE
WOOD PIT EXPLOSION ON 7TH JUNE 1878
WHO LIE AT REST ON THIS SITE

PLACED BY THE LANCASHIRE AREA N.U.M.
AND BRITISH COAL CORPORATION N.W. GROUP

Dedicated 7th June 1992
By The Rt. Revd. David Sheppard
Bishop Of Liverpool

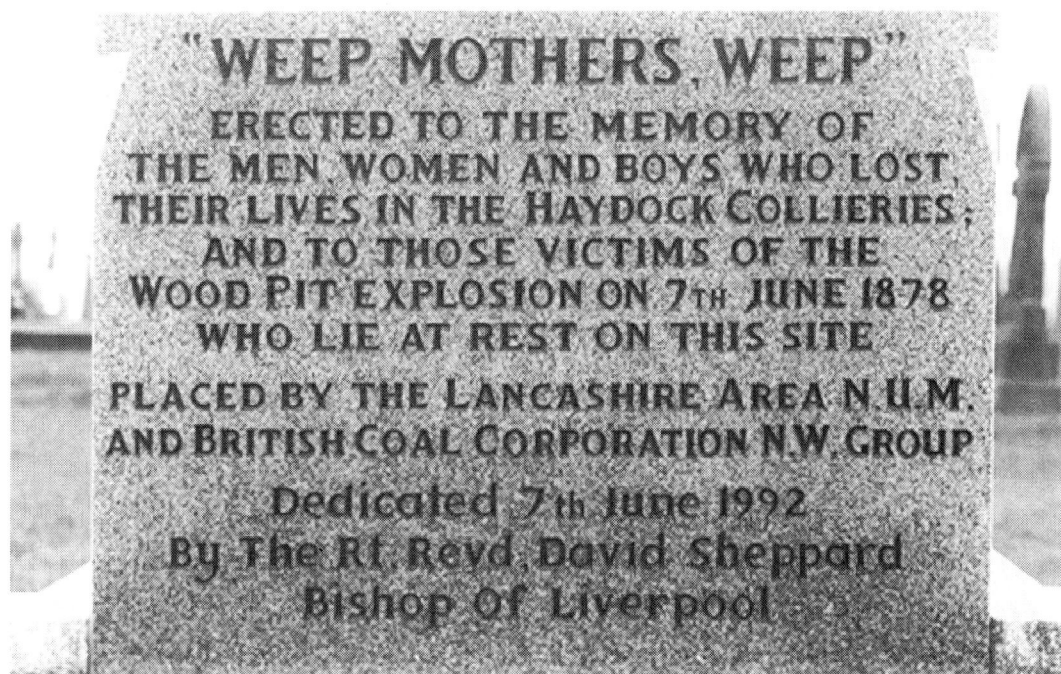

The Inscription.